D1396854

The
COST
of DOING
BUSINESS

The COST *of* DOING BUSINESS

**LEGAL AND REGULATORY ISSUES IN
THE UNITED STATES AND ABROAD**

PETER CHINLOY

PRAEGER

New York
Westport, Connecticut
London

Library of Congress Cataloging-in-Publication Data

Chinloy, Peter, 1950–
    The cost of doing business : legal and regulatory issues in the
United States and abroad / Peter Chinloy.
       p.   cm.
  Bibliography: p.
  ISBN 0-275-93332-6 (alk. paper)
  1. Industrial laws and legislation – United States. 2. Trade
regulation – United States. 3. Business enterprises – United States.
4. Industrial laws and legislation. 5. Trade regulation. 6. Costs,
Industrial.   I. Title.
KF1600.C46   1989
343.73'08 – dc19
[347.3038]   89-3650

Library of Congress Catalog Card Number: 89-3650
ISBN: 0-275-93332-6

First published in 1989

Praeger Publishers, One Madison Avenue, New York, NY 10010
A division of Greenwood Press, Inc.

Printed in the United States of America

The paper used in this book complies with the
Permanent Paper Standard issued by the National
Information Standards Organization (Z39.48-1984).

10 9 8 7 6 5 4 3 2 1

Contents

Tables

Acknowledgments

This project emerges from a concern by executives about their costs of doing business. These costs are not for production inputs similar across jurisdictions, such as the steel used in an automobile. Rather, there are differences in legal and regulatory costs entering as inputs in automobile production. The quantity of steel used in an automobile is itself the subject of regulatory and safety requirements. The concern is the level of cost imposed outside the firm, where the decision making is out of the hands of management.

The legal system in the United States has an effect on management decision making by imposing hidden costs. The senior executive spends time on activities imposed on the firm, such as responding to a lawsuit, as opposed to activities determined internally. Even if the firm reduces litigation by taking internal steps at quality control, these costs are mandated externally.

The project arose from discussions with A. C. (Mike) Markkula, vice chairman of Apple Computer, Cupertino, California, and owner of ACM Investments. He hypothesized that mandated costs, in reallocating the time of executives and other employees, were substantial. Despite the success of Apple Computer, and its products' low risk in liability, the firm spends considerable time on externally mandated legal and regulatory activity.

Mark Cleary, president of Clemco International, Burlingame, California, a manufacturer and supplier of construction equipment, had similar concerns and interests. Both have provided their own time to the project, and have cooperated with the research. David Clements, managing partner of the San Jose, California, office of the accounting firm of Arthur Andersen & Company, cooperated with the project.

The project was initiated in response to André Delbecq, Dean of the Leavey School of Business at Santa Clara University. I am grateful to Mike Gallagher for his research assistance throughout the project.

I am grateful to several persons for their cooperation with research. At Apple Computer, Albert Eisenstat, senior vice president, provided information on regulatory compliance and legal matters at the corporation. I had discussions and cooperation from the human resources and corporate counsel departments. As vice chairman of Apple Computer, Mike Markkula was instrumental in providing access. At Clemco International, I had the benefit of the advice and cooperation of Mark Cleary, president. Arthur Andersen has been helpful in providing data, through its Arthur Andersen Foundation, Chicago, and David Clements.

At the California Legal Reform Institute, Redwood City, California, Tom Skornia had many discussions on legal policy with me. I am grateful to U.S. Representative Tom Campbell of the Stanford Law School, and Deborah Bringelson, project manager of the Institute, for their cooperation. They have provided information on legal issues. I had discussions with staff at the Rand Corporation and Todd Stickle and other personnel at the National Center for State Courts.

On the cost of doing business in Japan, I had extensive discussions with Kazuo Koike of Kyoto University on the labor market. Tatsuo Tanase, professor of law, Kyoto University, has compared the legal systems of Japan and the United States. Carl Mosk provided information on various Japanese institutions.

I have received cooperation from the following organizations in providing information and data: Arthur Andersen Foundation, Chicago, access to staff professionals in their Delphi project, aimed at more complete accounting financial statements; Wyatt Company, Benefits Consultants, Chicago, data on directors' and officers' liability insurance, litigation, and health and benefit costs; Rand Institute of Civil Justice, Santa Monica, data on the total costs of maintaining the civil justice system; Manhattan Institute of Civil Justice, New York, research projects on the civil justice system in the United States; Brookings Institution, Washington, D.C., studies of the effect of regulation and deregulation; Japan Society, San Francisco, information on Japanese legal institutions; Jury Verdict Research, Inc., Solon, OH, information on civil litigation on product liability and wrongful termination suits; and National Center for State Courts, Williamsburg, VA, data on total civil litigation filed in state courts.

The
COST
of DOING
BUSINESS

1 Costs of Doing Business

INTRODUCTION AND SUMMARY

This project examines the externally imposed costs of doing business in a specific location. These include the costs of legal and regulatory compliance and of employee benefits. In economic analysis the costs of production are divided between capital and labor, supplemented by intermediate purchases from other firms and industries. To these has been added entrepreneurship.

All firms must comply with the legal system and regulatory requirements. Some firms are more efficient at compliance, and in operating within the legal system. Firms are nominally in the business of producing products, such as semiconductors or automobiles. Both also produce as outputs legal and regulatory services. There is variation in the degree of efficiency in producing these marketed outputs. Firms vary in their degree of interaction with the regulatory system. Drug and pharmaceutical firms are effectively captives of the system. This relationship works both ways. The firms are subject to regulation, but protected from outside competition. This study refers to the ability to absorb the costs associated with producing in a given location, and to use the institutions of the system profitably. Such activity requires the hiring of larger general and administrative (G&A) staff.

A principal conclusion is that externally imposed costs are higher for large firms than for small firms. This may explain why large firms have exhibited smaller growth rates in output and employment than smaller firms. Regulation and its enforcement are directed at larger firms. Large firms are more likely to be the objects of lawsuits and litigation. These firms carry more generous employee benefits, such as health care coverage for dependents.

Society determines the institutions and structure under which firms operate. If legal and accounting requirements oblige the firm to hire more lawyers and auditors, costs of production are higher. Suits against other firms and demands for increased regulation as protection are substitutes for reducing direct production costs.

EXTERNALLY IMPOSED AND HIDDEN COSTS

This research is on the hidden cost of doing business imposed externally on the firm. Costs are imposed not by productive considerations, but by the collective preferences of society. By the access price charged for the civil justice system, society determines the extent of litigation. Legislation determines the amount of regulation. Collective preference need not be reflected in litigation or regulation. If workers desire health benefits, firms in competitive markets provide them.

Firms employ legal staffs and other paper professionals to satisfy collective preferences. There are several potential consequences. The firm is restricted in capability to innovate. The directors and officers spend a portion of their time in response to litigation and regulation. The absolute competitiveness of firms is affected, since costs increase. Relative competitiveness is affected compared with countries not facing the same costs. The agenda of the firm is controlled externally rather than internally, and the flexibility to order priorities is restricted. Firms are less willing to take risks, since the cost of an error can be punitive.

A categorization of costs imposed on the firm is reported in Table 1.1. All costs are associated with collective preference in a specific location. Costs of litigation arise when access to a court system is priced lower in one jurisdiction than in another. Evidence is presented that the litigant against a corporation in the United States has a lower price of initiating charges than in competitive economies, notably Japan.

There are various conventions in allocating and dividing the costs of doing business. An accounting convention is to divide the costs between fixed and variable categories. Fixed costs include plant, equipment, and office personnel. Variable costs include raw materials and some production labor. An economic convention is to divide the

Table 1.1
Categories of Costs of Doing Business, Externally Imposed

Legal and litigation
        Product: goods: product liability
               services: professional malpractice
               intellectual property (patents/copyright)
               competitive practices
                    antitrust, dumping, trade practices
        Financial: debt - lender disputes
               equity - shareholder class actions
        Employees/ wrongful dismissal, employee termination
               discrimination
        Vendors: vendor disputes

Regulatory
        Product: safety and emission standards
               (Consumer Product Safety Commission)
               competitive practices
               (Federal Trade Commission)
               advertising (Truth in Advertising)
        Financial: debt - lender regulation, banking, monetary policy
               equity - securities regulation (Securities and
               Exchange Commission)
        Employees: occupational health and safety
               (Occupational Health and Safety Administration)
               employee hiring and grievances, affirmative action

Market
        Product: advertising, distribution channels
        Financial: equity - stock options, Employee Stock Ownership
               Programs (under stock market randomness)
        Employees: health care and medical benefits, pensions

costs between capital and labor. Capital costs are payments for plant and equipment, and labor costs for human resources used in production.

Neither classification takes account of whether the firm incurs the costs voluntarily, or whether they are imposed from outside. Some costs are imposed by collective preference, as reflected through the judiciary, the legislature, or the market. The firm can avoid costs by shifting to a new jurisdiction. Steel is required to produce cars in all locations. Litigation support is either not required, or there is variation in its requirement across locations.

More importantly, some of these costs are hidden, and do not appear on financial statements. Time is spent by executives on litigation and regulation when they are not specifically assigned to those tasks. Resources are diverted from other activities.

These costs are not directly related to production. A firm producing in the United States has a plant safety regulation not present in Japan, but the two producers sell in the same market. The firm in the United States has an imposed cost of doing business that cannot be shifted to the consumer.

Involuntary costs are those imposed from outside, not necessarily by government edict. Some, such as compliance with pollution control regulations, are a consequence of legislation. Others, such as the cost of litigation, arise from legislation regarding access to publicly provided courts.

Other costs are imposed by competitive conditions in the market. A firm may not be able to offer benefits such as health insurance. Competitors offer such programs, and the employer risks losing employees if it fails to match benefits. The employer frequently has little or no control over the level of usage of these benefits. Indirect costs arise with administration of benefit programs. Some employees receive cross-subsidies in cost that cannot be shifted to the remainder of the work force.

The three types of externally imposed costs are distinguished as judicial, regulatory, and market. The firm bears costs in these three categories as observed on financial statements under generally accepted accounting practice (GAAP). The cost of paying for liability insurance, or of an employee benefit plan, are included as expenditures. In the accounting framework, liability insurance is a part of overhead. In the economic framework, employee benefits are a part of labor costs. These costs could be reduced if production took place in another jurisdiction.

Collective preferences, through the judiciary, the legislature, and the market, have other consequences for costs. These costs need not be measured under GAAP. Such hidden costs include the effect on the time of senior executives. The health benefits manager is a common position in the United States, but is unlikely to be found in Western Europe. The cost of this position is directly ascribable to collective preference, as are much of the legal, accounting, and financial departments. Externally imposed costs include some GAAP expenditures on these employees.

The measurement problem becomes more acute for nondedicated employees, whose jobs entail switching between various tasks. Some of these tasks may be imposed externally. This problem affects nonspecialized managers, officers, and directors. There are hidden costs. A manager finds that a portion of time is spent on legal or regulatory compliance.

The firm increases general and administrative (G&A) expenditure. The employee with a graduate business degree serves as a flexible manager, assignable to various tasks. Alternatively, this employee is required because form filling adds layers of paper professionals. Paper professionals include actuaries, accountants, lawyers, graduate business degree holders, and financial analysts. Some of these workers are required without external mandate. The demand becomes larger to satisfy externally imposed compliance. The task is to develop a structure capable of analyzing the direct and hidden costs of compliance.

IMPOSED COSTS: CONSEQUENCES

Risk Acceptance

One consequence of being penalized on liability is that firms are less willing to innovate, and to invest in new products. Firms are more risk averse in product development. With the reduced risk taking comes an increase in the defensive posture of the firm. It moves into a reactive mode, responding to external pressure rather than innovating internally.

A refrigerator is a dangerous product. It poses a risk of a child trapped by a locked door, unable to escape. The manufacturer, knowing the risk of such a tragedy, improves the capacity of the refrigerator to be unlocked from the inside. The cost of improvements and litigation are part of the price of the refrigerator. The manufacturer may chafe at these costs. It could be argued that the premium is high if the manufacturer does not agree with the expected payment awarded for accidents. Payments differ across societies and affect the prices of refrigerators.

A more difficult problem arises when the product is used for a purpose for which it is not intended. Suppose there is a race to determine who can carry a refrigerator strapped to the back the longest. An accident ensues, and damages are awarded against the manufacturer of the refrigerator. Under strict liability, an accident with an injury is compensable against the manufacturer. The manufacturer cannot necessarily foresee the usage, but includes a reserve to cover these liability costs. The level of judicially imposed costs is greater than otherwise.

The price of access to the legal system determines usage. The potential plaintiff includes an expected return from a settlement in assessing whether to purchase a good or service. The supplier includes not only production but legal costs for defense, and payments to counsel for the plaintiff. There are internal costs to the firm, such as reallocation of time, and increasing staff on compliance. A differential arises between the net return to the claimant and the cost to the supplier. The larger this differential is, the greater the distortion in the prices of products.

International Competitiveness

These differences in cost affect international competitiveness. Producers from two countries selling in the same market are both vulnerable to the given liability environment. Japanese and U.S. producers have the same product liability rules in the American market. The distributor of the Japanese product in the United States is located a long distance from the plant. Because of the higher cost of repairs due to distance, the Japanese firm has an incentive to develop products with lower failure rates and fault tolerance. This characteristic arises from an inherent market condition, and not collective preferences. Distance from the market generates cost differences.

Distance is not the only characteristic distinguishing jurisdictions. The Japanese plant is subject to a different set of collective preferences. Regulations on health and safety differ between the United States and Japan. The producer in the United States has the more accessible legal system, and costs of employee grievances and wrongful dismissal that do not arise in Japan.

Flexibility and Delegation

The legal system causes management to reorganize priorities. Responses to legal actions require immediate attention, regardless of the economic cost associated with them. The degree of flexibility of management is reduced because priorities on the corporate agenda are dictated from outside, by the judicial system. The executive cannot be engaged in strategic planning on new products if a reply on a legal matter is demanded immediately.

The legal system frequently prevents delegation of responsibility. If the chief executive officer (CEO) is named in a legal action together with the firm, personal liability arises. The CEO can be required to be present in court proceedings, without being able to delegate this function. The CEO is obliged to be familiar with the details of legal proceedings, a briefing process that comes at the expense of other production and development activity.

Personal liability for the actions of a corporation on the part of officers and directors has other implications. Firms must carry directors' and officers' (D&O) liability insurance. This cost is an added expenditure of doing business, together with the costs of legal awards and counsel. An individual desiring to be a director, with relatively low remuneration, can be liable in an action against that corporation. Outside directors come at a higher price, and with greater reluctance.

The firm is a less flexible entity. Some of its activities are mandated from outside, and officers who are not dedicated to compliance tasks must reorder their priorities.

In litigation, the firm and its officers face negative publicity, even if successful either in having litigation dismissed or settling. There may be a psychological aspect to being accused of guilt that makes individuals reluctant to accept risk. This psychological aspect could affect job performance and relations with family and community. The firm, its directors, and officers are distracted. The firm is vulnerable to attacks on market share, to a failure to introduce new products, and to takeover from outside.

Research and Development

The bias in research and development has been alluded to in product liability. There is an increase in the amount of testing for new products, because the risk of failure is punished by collective preferences, acting through the civil justice system. There is a risk of punitive damages. Since the firm does not wish to cross-subsidize any punitive damages from other products, an additional cost is built into research and development.

Barriers to Entry

The cost of defending in the judicial system is frequently substantial. For products with a risk of personal injury, such as pharmaceuticals, only relatively deep-pocketed firms carry the liability risk. Risky products are introduced by relatively large firms, with smaller firms less likely to innovate. The capacity of smaller firms to innovate in areas entailing personal risk is limited. Large firms are cautious, if the risk of punitive damages extends beyond a specific product.

COSTS IMPOSED BY THE JUDICIAL SYSTEM

Introduction

Access to the legal system is determined by collective preference. Alternative methods exist for settling civil disputes, such as arbitration, where both sides select a neutral third party, and the cost is divided between the disputants.

The public is affected by disputes between individuals. If a product is defective, society has an interest in making it safer. The judicial system, by imposing penalties on unsafe products, creates incentives for increasing safety.

In any market, access is determined by the price charged. There is limited control on the time spent on a case. The individual who brings a legal action bears a negligible portion of the total cost. With widespread access to the legal system, the costs are shifted to taxpayers other than the litigants. The decision-making litigant pays low filing fees. Legal counsel is retained on a contingency basis, with payment upon settlement. For incurring these fees, the litigant obtains court time paid for by society, with little restriction on the level of use. There is leverage in legal action. The litigant considers only the low private costs, though the cost to business and society are large. This leverage and low cost to the initiator increase litigation.

Litigiousness

Litigiousness is reflected in the proportion of lawyers in the population and relative expenditure on civil justice. There is an asymmetric information exchange between lawyer and client. The asymmetry arises because the lawyer is better informed about the legal system than the client. An increase in the supply of lawyers can increase the demand for legal services and litigation.

Because asymmetric information can increase the quantity of litigation, it has been proposed that entry to the legal profession should be limited, to reduce the supply-driven demand for litigation. On the supply side, the cost of producing an additional lawyer is small. This cost is unlike that of a medical school, where research and laboratory facilities are required. The cost of adding one student to a law school class is largely a class seat, since the major expenses of a library and faculty are fixed.

Another method of restricting entry is to raise passing scores on bar exams. This protects entrenched members, with the entire adjustment borne by new entrants. The relatively low cost of entering the legal profession, combined with large rewards, entails a large supply of lawyers, and increased litigation. Any reduction in the numbers in law schools takes time to have an effect on the existing stock of lawyers.

Product Markets

Access to the legal system imposes costs in the product market. Product liability costs vary across jurisdictions, depending on the preferences of society for access to the courts. The costs are not necessarily driven by a desire for compensation for an injured party. There may be more efficient methods for such delivery.

Certain aspects of product liability affect the degree and magnitude of lawsuits. Apart from general litigiousness, these include punitive damages, strict liability, deep pockets, contingency fees, class actions, and allocation of costs.

Punitive damages discourage firms from producing unsafe products. They are awarded in addition to economic losses suffered by a claimant. They punish and deter reprehensible behavior. Strict liability awards damages when a user suffers an injury, regardless of fault. Deep pockets, or joint and several liability, provides that a defendant with partial responsibility can be liable for all the costs of an award. Contingency fees to attorneys are paid as a percentage of an award or settlement. Class action lawsuits are filed on behalf of a large number of claimants.

The division of costs between litigants depends on legal institutions. In the United States, the plaintiff, even if unsuccessful, is not liable for attorney fees of the defendant. The defendant is liable to cover the costs of the successful plaintiff.

The direct costs of litigation are insurance, the size of the corporate legal department, and the costs of settlements. There are indirect costs of reduced research on new products, and in the distraction of senior management.

Products are more expensive because of the costs of product liability. The problem arises particularly with medical products. Product liability has increased the cost of the DPT vaccine against diphtheria, pertussis (whooping cough), and tetanus. Some producers of the vaccine, such as American Home Products, have withdrawn from the market because of the added cost of liability insurance. Other products being withdrawn from U.S. markets include anesthesia machines.

It is not necessarily inappropriate that a product has 80 percent or more of its cost in liability or legal costs. Thalidomide caused birth defects in Europe. Problems arise with intrauterine devices. A similar argument applies to the removal of products from the market. Certain products are inherently unsafe or risky. Some products, notably pharmaceuticals, require large initial quantities of research, development, and testing.

Society could obtain the same protection for victims and claimants through less expensive delivery vehicles. There is a transactions cost gap between the expenses of a defendant and the net return to a plaintiff. The plaintiff and defendant can benefit through alternative dispute resolution.

With any drug, there is a risk of illness and side effects to the user, and another risk of not treating potential users. Litigation is concerned with the former. Damages are awarded against the manufacturer to penalize harmful side effects. Those not receiving a treatment because it is not on the market have limited access to the legal system. The legal system causes firms to be more cautious and averse to risk. This aversion is privately optimal, given the cost of a mistake. The error of not having a treatment available in the drug industry increases.

The balance between the suffering of users and the suffering of non-users depends on collective preferences. Society loses when a product is not available. Given the risk of litigation, the firm has an incentive to delay development. Only society loses, since the firm is responding optimally, given the legal environment.

Financial Markets

The legal system affects firms in their costs of financial services. Financial activities include dealings with lenders on the debt side and with shareholders on the equity side.

Where the prospect of litigation is higher, the amount of cost and paperwork to avoid such action is higher. There is an insistence that agreements between a firm and lenders be in writing, supervised by lawyers, to cover possibilities such as breach of contract. The cost of access is reduced by low court filing fees and contingency fees to lawyers for plaintiffs. This low cost increases litigation, as opposed to arbitration, in resolving disputes. A handshake or gentlemen's agreement where one's word is honored may arise because the cost of alternative dispute resolution is high. In Japan, where lawyers are less common than in the United States, there is pressure to honor verbal agreements.

Lenders have a prior claim from earnings for interest and principal repayment. Shareholders do not. Their equity position is protected by the opportunity to litigate. Developments in equity markets permit investors to hold long or short positions in common stock and other claims against a public corporation. Widely traded issues have put and call options providing rights respectively to sell and buy the common stock.

The cost of a stock price decline is not only a capital loss for investors but the risk of legal action against directors and officers. The response of the public corporation takes various forms. First, there is a tendency to become private, or to reduce the outstanding float of common stock. Second, directors and officers take steps to minimize fluctuation in the short-run stock price, regardless of the long-term implications. Third, there is an incentive to move headquarters to a jurisdiction where litigation is restricted. Delaware has favorable corporate civil laws. Alternatively, the firm moves the core of its headquarters overseas. There are increases in legal risk, and higher insurance premiums for directors' and officers' (D&O) liability. The indirect cost is the distraction of directors and officers from productive activity, and toward the defensive posture required in litigation.

Foreign competitors, headquartered overseas, may be able to avoid these costs. If the legal environment in Japan and West Germany is more restricted than in the United States, the costs associated with shareholder litigation are lower.

While the firm has direct line item costs for litigation settlement and lawyers, there are indirect costs. The time of the directors in a public corporation is occupied with legal matters not arising for private or overseas competitors. Executives act more cautiously, with an eye to the daily gyrations of stock prices.

Employees and Vendors

The difference in competitiveness is increased in markets for purchased inputs, such as labor, machinery, and intermediate inputs. Differences in costs of production arise across locations and jurisdictions, although competitors are selling in the same market. Firms selling in a market do not have to produce in that market. Input litigation concerns relations of a firm with its employees, suppliers, and vendors. One area is the cost of defense, settlement, and the indirect cost of documentation and time in employee dismissal. In the United States, unlike West Germany and Japan, there is less tendency for a worker to be attached to a firm. Collective preferences for job security impose restrictions on laying off workers in Germany. Bilateral implicit agreements in Japan reinforce loyalty and tenure of employees.

A worker dismissed for any reason may bring a civil action for damages against a former employer. The firm must document a history and chain of events prior to dismissal. Even though a firm is not prohibited by law or custom from dismissing a worker, collective preferences increase the cost of grievance procedures, and of settling wrongful dismissal actions. Firms retain workers who are unproductive, since the cost of firing is higher than of continuing to employ.

If a court makes an award compensating a dismissed worker for a long period, there is an explicit notion that the employee would have had a long-term attachment. Society regards the employee as having a capital investment in the firm. There is little practical distinction between a long tenure and a short tenure plus termination and separation payments. If costs of dismissal increase due to compensation over a longer period, the firm has less incentive to remove unproductive employees.

As the costs of employee grievances increase, firms hire fewer workers and increase their capital intensity. They are cautious in hiring, particularly in large firms with deep pocket risk. There is an incentive to seek locations less restrictive in the allocation and utilization of labor.

The costs of termination, in awards and settlement, are reallocated among remaining workers. More labor- and skill-intensive firms suffer relatively, but the costs of doing business for all employers are increased.

The firm purchases supplies from vendors and other contributors of intermediate inputs. Disputes arise with landlords, suppliers of raw materials, and equipment that fails or does not work as promised. The same principle as for product liability arises, except that the firm is potentially a plaintiff. The firm cannot collect for emotional pain and suffering, but is eligible for punitive damages, and damages for the economic loss. The accessibility of the legal system makes it a favored channel for disputes. Where the costs to the claimant are low, the legal system is a first rather than last resort. Handshakes and living up to one's word are more costly than using legal remedies.

COSTS IMPOSED BY REGULATION

Collective preferences are expressed in government regulation. There are direct and indirect costs of regulation; the latter do not appear on GAAP financial statements.

Regulations affecting products include standards, labelling, and control of pollutants. Society benefits if products adhere to standards, reducing search and comparison time by consumers. Labelling permits consumers to become informed about products, and to make choices efficiently. Emission controls reduce effluent in the air, land, and water. These benefits arise to society. The costs are in the prices charged to consumers.

Products are made more expensive by regulation. If a car must be equipped with a catalytic converter to reduce effluent discharge, its price is increased. Some regulations, such as on emissions, require fixed investments per car. The price of cheaper cars is increased relative to expensive cars. Automobiles are less available to poorer people. The cost-benefit analysis of a regulation requires accounting for income distribution effects.

Part of the cost-benefit analysis is any indirect impact, such as the cost of distraction of executives. If a firm is required to provide reports on labelling, or to hire additional inspectors, these are costs of regulation.

COSTS IMPOSED BY MARKETS

A third category of socially imposed costs arises from the market. These costs are culturally imposed, or created by an absence of public provision. An important category is for medical care. General Motors estimates that in 1987 employee medical costs accounted for $500 for each car produced in the United States. Cars produced in Canada, where there is public provision of health care, carry a negligible medical cost. The price of medical care has increased more rapidly than prices in general. The quantity of care utilization has increased more rapidly than real gross national product.

In the United States medical costs are paid by employers. The individual employee is the decision maker on usage. One hypothesis is that when confronted with medical information that the patient is unable to interpret, there is deference to the specialist. The patient is willing to accept treatment suggestions of the physician that can increase costs. Cost controls, including surgical second opinions, and restricting choice of providers, limit freedoms and rights to privacy. The employee-patient and physician are the decision makers. The firm and its insurer are third parties, paying the bills, but with limited controls on usage, demand, or pricing.

Market preferences affect the benefits packages offered to employees. Benefits include paid tuition, life insurance, food concessions, parking, travel, pensions, and health insurance. Employers offer benefits because of favorable tax treatment. The firm deducts employee benefit expenses from revenue in calculating corporate taxable income. The employee excludes benefits from current taxable income. Except for pensions, it is possible for the employee never to include benefits in any taxable income. The employee prefers one dollar of cash to one dollar of benefits, were they equally taxed. The dollar of benefits is restricted in usage, while the dollar of cash is restricted. The reduced or nonexistent taxes on benefits leads to an increased demand for them.

Some benefits have economies of scale. The advantage of the firm as bulk purchaser reduces transaction costs of insurance, either for life or health. Transaction costs include marketing the insurance and the paperwork for each customer. Employees have common characteristics that produce more favorable risks for an insurer. They are employed, and the reliability of the firm is translated into reduced premiums. The economies of scale result in lower prices to employees than if they were to purchase insurance on the open market.

While taxes and economies of scale are reasons to offer benefits, the fundamental reason arises from collective preference. Employees desire the security provided by pensions and health benefits. No government legislation is needed to mandate benefits. The market, rather than the judiciary or the legislature, acts as the delivery vehicle for the collective preferences.

Benefits programs become an externally imposed cost. While a firm can legally not offer health insurance, it risks losing workers to competitors. There are both direct and hidden costs from benefits programs.

CONCLUDING REMARKS

Regulation takes two forms, either as police power or in administrative procedures. With police power, the regulatory agency enforces rules, and punishes firms breaking them. Administrative procedures involve the regulatory agency allocating and dividing markets, and arbitrating disputes between firms. Regulatory agencies in the United States exhibit police power. They are concerned less with allocation of output than with the consequences, such as monopolies. In Japan, regulatory agencies and the Ministry of International Trade and Industry carry out administrative procedures. There is a natural antagonism between business and government in a police power environment.

In the United States certain institutions, notably courts and regulatory agencies, are expensive to use but not to the user. Access to litigation and tribunals is possible at low entry fees. Legal compensation, in contingency fees, permits low-cost access to claimants. By comparison, Western European nations and Japan do not permit contingency fees. The institutions of the United States facilitate access and preserve the freedom to make contracts. Third-party payment implies that the decision maker, as disputant, does not take into account the total cost of actions.

The low access cost implies that the claimant has leverage. The cost is shifted to the taxpayer, in agencies and the courts. The cost is shifted to firms when they defend against actions, since they are unable to recover defense costs. A conflict arises in the use of public institutions to settle private disputes. The beneficiaries are individual or corporate disputants.

2 Externally Imposed Costs: The Law, Regulation, and the Market

This project originated with two observations by executives of successful companies in the Silicon Valley, Santa Clara County, California, a hotbed of innovative and entrepreneurial development in the United States. The first is that a large amount of time is spent on litigation. The principal types of litigation are on financial disputes, product liability, and employee grievances. Another firm indicates that throughout its history, total net claims in lawsuits exceeded the value of its net assets.

The second observation is that a portion of total costs are not related to production, but mandated by public legislation or contractual behavior. Such costs include environmental and safety standards.

The two types of costs, for litigation and mandated public policy, have an indirect effect on a firm. This cost arises because the chief executive officer (CEO) and senior management must be involved in the response to outside claims. The chairman of Chrysler Corporation notes, "Most of the letters I usually get from lawyers start out, 'You are hereby summoned,' and lined up with 'ignore at your own peril.'"[1] The delegation of responsibility normally associated with a corporate structure does not apply.

Another phenomenon of United States business is an increase in the proportion of employees engaged in services, as opposed to goods production. In the white-collar sector, corporations recruit accountants, lawyers, those with graduate business degrees, and other professional workers, in addition to support staffs. Other countries, potentially competitors, have relatively few of these professional service workers. Are these workers hired to increase the productivity of the firm, or is their relative employment a consequence of the business environment?

The objective is to examine the costs of production mandated externally. The focus is on senior executives, and how they and other employees spend their time. This chapter summarizes the entire study, and presents some hypotheses to be examined.

The key notion is contained in the title, *The Cost of Doing Business*. The principal externally imposed costs for the U.S. firm are associated with litigation, regulatory compliance, and employee benefits. These cost categories are not exhaustive. Rather, they present a categorization of the problems facing corporations.

The core hypothesis is as follows. Externally mandated costs are higher in the United States than in competitive countries. Location decisions are made on the basis of externally mandated costs, even where direct production costs and the technology are similar. Within the United States, external costs vary across jurisdictions. A director or officer, in addition to the corporation, can be named as personally liable in litigation. There is an opportunity cost of the executive being in a reactive mode, as opposed to an innovative one.

Firms are defensive and less innovative in their product and service development. Products with a risk are removed from the market. Ultimately, research and development is moved to locations where externally imposed costs are lower.

Firms hire white-collar staff, in legal and accounting departments, and relatively fewer in research and engineering. It is more profitable to avoid costs of regulation and litigation. The hiring of these paper professionals is justifiable, given the cost structure of the firm. Their employment might be reduced in another jurisdiction. Such cost avoidance can be more profitable than with new products. Location is based on direct production costs, and on indirect mandated costs.

External costs are based on social as opposed to private cost-benefit calculations. An injured user receives compensation from the manufacturer. Society benefits if pollution of the air, land, and water is reduced. The problem is that costs are not necessarily borne in the manner in which they were inflicted. A firm polluting groundwater imposes a cost on society. It is not unreasonable to ask for a cleanup. The firm has an externally imposed increase in its cost, but it had previously been inflicting the cost on society. The matter becomes more nebulous when a firm is subject to generic liability. Under liability for a generic product, a claimant collects damages from a well-known producer even if its product cannot be unequivocally shown to have been used.

TYPES OF COSTS

The costs have been divided into three categories. In the first group are costs arising from public policy access, notably to the judicial system. These are imposed indirectly by legislation on court access.

In the second category are costs imposed by governments. These include costs of regulatory compliance and pollution control. They are directly imposed by collective preference.

In the third category are imposed competitive costs. These are not required by law. Markets for employees and customers oblige the firm to incur these costs or risk losses to competitors. Examples lie in employee benefits. The firm cannot easily reallocate costs such as for medical care among all workers. The firm absorbs them as a hidden or indirect cost. Externally imposed costs are mandated outside the firm, not directly related to production. The test for an externally imposed cost is that it is avoidable by switching the location of production or sale.

Litigation and Legal

The firm responds to the judicial structure by the size of the legal department, both in-house and in the retention of outside counsel. Costs are imposed by the settlement of suits and proceedings, and by insurance premium payments. The level of senior executive staff is increased because of legal issues. The CEO is obliged to spend a portion of the work day on legal problems.

Legal issues have been divided into three categories: product, financial, and input or vendor. Product liability claims affect suppliers of goods and services. The producer of a good invests in quality assurance and control to reduce liability costs. Within a state or municipality, suppliers must adhere to the laws governing product liability, including personal responsibility of the directors and officers.

There are differences in costs facing suppliers, particularly under judicial rules such as strict liability. Under strict liability, injuries are compensable against a defendant, with no proof of fault required. The alternative to strict liability is contributory negligence. Under contributory negligence, fault is apportioned between plaintiff and defendant. A U.S. domestic producer has lower costs of transportation and support supplying the U.S. market than an overseas producer. The overseas producer has an incentive to reduce the costs of service or other product recalls. Otherwise, the overseas supplier is obliged to maintain service staffs and parts distribution networks. This incentive arises from the market, with no judicial intervention.

The presence of tight judicial standards on product liability add to the relative disadvantage of the U.S. producer. The costs of transportation and a service network alone can justify an overseas supplier optimally investing in improved quality control, as compared with the domestic competitor. The domestic producer is penalized further by facing higher liability costs. Some of these liability costs relate to inputs and production, avoided by the overseas supplier.

Product liability legislation increases the costs of producing goods and services for export. The overseas user has access to U.S. product liability legislation and the court system. To provide some restriction of foreign access to U.S. tribunals, the Supreme Court has permitted federal district courts to use the doctrine of *forum non conveniens*. Under this doctrine, a case should be tried in a jurisdiction convenient to claimants and witnesses and to documents of the case. The doctrine usually rejects foreign claimants' access to U.S. courts, but not in all cases. Foreigners are able to use the accessible court services provided by U.S. taxpayers in legal actions against U.S. companies. The costs of exporting to overseas markets become larger for U.S. suppliers. They have a liability for legal expenses for overseas buyers.

Financial liability includes litigation with lenders, shareholders, venture capital suppliers, and providers of other than physical assets and liabilities. Shareholder litigation is facilitated by class action lawsuits. The owner of 100 shares in a company whose stock price declines from $20 to $10 has lost $1,000. This sum is insufficient to hire a lawyer for a day, let alone pay filing costs. If shareholders are grouped into a class, the potential liability of the corporation expands.

In a class action, the firm has costs in defending, including the penalty in the multiplier paid for plaintiffs' attorney fees. Under the multiplier rule, the defendant pays legal fees of plaintiffs' attorneys at several times the prevailing rate. The rationale for the multiplier in class actions is twofold. First, each member of the class individually stands to gain little from litigation, given transaction costs. There are economies of scale in pooling litigants. Second, there is a risk to the plantiffs' attorney in bringing a class action case.

Shareholder lawsuits create an incentive for public corporations to become private. The benefit to being a public corporation lies in the ability of owners to have a market for their equity without selling control of the firm. Managers sell their equity without losing their jobs. The cost is from the watchdog effect of the market. The firm is under pressure to produce short-term success.[2] The risk of shareholder lawsuits against the firm, director, and officers is another cost. Firms whose shares are not publicly traded or foreign competitors whose headquarters are abroad, do not have the same costs of shareholder litigation.

To guard against disputes, the documentation required to close financial arrangements has increased. Lenders risk suits for breach of contract from borrowers denied funding. Financial transactions in less litigious environments are decided by a handshake, or with a reduced paperwork burden.

On the input side, legal costs arise with employee grievances and in disputes with vendors. Employee discharges are subject to litigation. There are disputes with and suits for discrimination and affirmative action. Some of these cases are meritorious and appropriately compensable. However, overseas producers do not have similar costs for litigation or employee grievances. Disputes with vendors, or suppliers of products, materials, equipment, and plant, place the firm as plaintiff or defendant. The same considerations apply as for product liability disputes. The liability issues are summarized in Table 2.1.

Regulatory Compliance

Society establishes regulations both to increase efficiency and equity, and to govern the operation of markets. Firms are regulated in output markets on health, safety, and the environment. In financial markets, debt and equity are regulated. Debt issues are subject to banking and monetary policy. Equity issues involve securities laws. The financial statements are subject to both tax laws and conformity with accounting standards. In input markets there are environmental, health, and safety standards for plant, equipment, vendor purchases, and labor. The response to a regulatory agency, as with a court, is required to be immediate, and frequently cannot be delegated.

The benefits of regulation accrue to society, through a cleaner and

Table 2.1
Litigation Costs and Potential Effects on Domestic and Foreign Producers

	Domestic Producer	Foreign Producer
Product Liability		
Domestic Market	Affected	Affected, but less
Foreign Market	Affected (foreign access to U.S. Torts)	Not affected
Financial		
Shareholders	Affected if public company	Less affected if private or foreign[a]
Lenders	Affected	Not affected if no domestic borrowing
Input		
Employee	Affected	Less affected (only on domestic employees)
Vendors/Suppliers	Affected (if production offshore)	Less affected

[a]Some foreign producers issue stock in the United States as American Deposit Receipts (ADRs), with claims against the shares. ADR holders may have rights of litigation, but if they are a small percentage of the total, there are practical difficulties in pooling all shareholders. Shareholder class actions usually exclude ADR stocks.

safer workplace and environment. Regulation in potentially hazardous products, such as pharmaceuticals, reduces the risk of side effects. Where consumers are unable to make fully informed choices, quick cures are kept off the market. There are costs of regulation. Firms and organizations subject to regulation have direct costs of compliance. Investment in scrubbers to reduce sulfuric emissions for smokestacks has no payoff in increased output, but a social return in a cleaner environment. Firms have indirect costs, in executive time allocated to regulatory compliance. Such costs, if excluded from the social cost-benefit calculation, lead to a higher than socially optimal level of regulation. Costs arise for Type II errors, where the regulatory delay in approval of a drug causes additional illness. Regulation prevents the Type I error, of side effects in the use of a drug.

The scope of regulation is broad, and covers product markets, inputs, health and safety, and environmental concerns. To focus attention, the effect of regulation here has narrowed. Since current interest is in the high-technology sector, general issues of regulation that affect these firms are addressed. Producers of computers, semiconductors, and software have a substantially different regulatory environment than biotechnology producers. Since biotechnology firms are highly regulated, this sector is examined in detail as a case study.

In product markets, emissions and product safety are regulated. Litigation acts as a complement to regulation, with product liability and malpractice cases. Industrial safety and work rules are also regulated. An unsafe work environment, or exposure to toxics that are not regulated increases employee grievances and litigation. Financial regulation includes accounting and auditing, dealings with shareholders on the equity side, and with lenders on the debt side. Litigation emerges from shareholder lawsuits. Table 2.2 compares domestic and foreign producers on regulation, when both sell in the domestic market.

Market-Imposed (Competitive) Costs

Litigation and regulation measure the effect of collective preference. Hidden costs arise other than in distraction of the CEO and other executives. Competition and markets oblige firms to incur costs where there is no clear return in output. Employee benefits are examples of market-imposed costs. These benefits are not tied to the individual productivity of the worker. This external imposition comes from the rules of the market, some of which are set by regulation.

Some competitive, large firms offer full benefits. Smaller firms offer fewer benefits, and enjoy a free ride on the packages of large firms, which find it difficult to expand employment. Between 1980 and 1987, employment at the largest U.S. firms — the Fortune 500 — decreased by 3 million people, while total employment in the economy increased by 15 million. While other factors are at work, health and other benefits are part of the cost of business at large firms; these benefits are usually more limited in small firms.

Pension Plans

Pension provisions, either by regulation or by custom, prevent a lower payment to a retiree, even where there are differences in mortality. A

Table 2.2
**Regulatory Compliance Costs and Potential Effects on Domestic
and Foreign Producers**

	Domestic Producer	Foreign Producer
Product		
Health/Safety	Affected	Affected
Financial		
Shareholders	Affected in public	Less affected if private or foreign
Lenders	Affected	Not affected if no domestic borrowing
Input		
Employee	Affected	Less affected, only domestic employees
Vendors/Suppliers	Affected	Not affected, if produced offshore

firm has a male and a female worker of equal productivity, age, and experience. The two workers are paid the same compensation. Their productivity on the job is the same. The firm operates a defined benefit pension plan, where the payment to a retiree is stipulated and guaranteed. The female employee has a longer life expectancy after retirement age. Where the pension plan provides a defined benefit, the expected duration of the payment is not taken into account. The expected present values of payments to male and female employees differ. There is a larger pension obligation to the female with the longer life expectancy.

Defined benefit pension plans are typical in the public sector, at federal, state, and local government levels. They are present in old-line manufacturing sectors such as steel and automobiles. While governments are able to absorb the costs of defined benefit plans, or to shift them to taxpayers, private firms are not. The plans were put in place before there was a high percentage of women eligible for retirement benefits. The firm cannot reduce the compensation of the male worker, to cover its loss on hiring the female worker. It cannot easily reduce the current salary of the female worker, nor can it reduce the pension benefits. It cannot introduce a policy of reducing female hires. It has a cost that cannot be shifted to other employees. The male worker shares the cost, if the firm reduces current compensation for all workers. Compensation for males and females is reduced to cover the anticipated loss on the pension account. The firm shifts its loss to the employees. Alternatively, the firm has a hidden cost of subsidizing certain workers.

Some of these problems are removed by tying benefits more closely to current compensation. Current compensation reflects the actual value of the employee to the firm. For retirement benefits, the firm offers a defined contribution pension plan. There is no guarantee as to the ultimate pension receipt of the employee. The firm contributes to the pension fund based on the current earnings of the employee. The firm has either no pension plan or a limited plan. Additional compensation takes the form of a bonus or stock options.

Health and Medical Care

The fraction of the gross national product spent on medical care has increased from 7 percent in the early 1960s to over 12 percent in the late 1980s. Despite this expenditure, aggregate health services are not more favorable than in Western Europe. In countries such as Britain, health costs are considerably lower as a share of total output. In Western Europe, Canada, and Japan, health care costs are paid by direct taxes. The firm does not pay health care costs of individual employees, or single illness claims. Because direct tax and payroll tax rates are higher in Europe, it is conceivable that health care costs are neutral, as compared with the United States. In the United States the employer bears the cost directly through health care premiums. In Western Europe, Canada, and Japan the employer bears the cost indirectly, through payroll and income taxes. Workers in the United States and other industrial nations receive comparable health care benefits. Only the method of financing differs. The CEO is typically not directly involved in the administration of health care. Channels of delegation are permitted to operate.

However, health care is not necessarily neutral, because the cost of provision is larger in the United States than in countries where it is publicly provided. Plants of automobile manufacturers in Canada operate without the health care cost burden of the United States. The three U.S. manufacturers, General Motors, Ford, and Chrysler, have expanded Canadian production, assisted by the Canadian–U.S. Auto Pact of 1964. This pact provides for free trade in automobiles between the two countries. They are being joined by greenfield plants for Toyota and Hyundai, where the principal objective is access to the U.S. market. The health cost advantage alone makes location of manufacturing production in Canada attractive.

Few corporations in Western Europe, Canada, or Japan require a department for negotiating with health insurance carriers. There is less need for a benefits management department, as large a personnel department, or outside benefits consultants.

Employees demand health care because of the possibility of catastrophic bills and the risk of loss of income. There is no universal public provision of health care in the United States. National average is limited to two target groups. Those over 65 in Medicare, and the poor in Medicaid receive public health care. The firm not offering health care, particularly hiring skilled employees, risks losing workers to another employer. Competitive conditions oblige the firm to offer health care benefits to its employees. At Hewlett-Packard in 1987, health care expenditures were $100 million for 54,000 employees in the United States, or about $2,000 per employee on average. This average cost is similar to that paid by all U.S. companies. The company must sell at the retail price, well above the wholesale price received as revenue, over 20 of its most popular calculators to pay the health costs of one employee. Meanwhile, a firm in Singapore offers no health benefits, and one in Canada has them provided publicly.

The hidden cost on a firm is greater if the health plan covers dependents. Consider two employees of equal productivity. One has no dependents, and the other has five dependents. The employees have the same health status. The employee with five dependents imposes a higher health cost. If the workers have the same productivity and job, the firm cannot reduce the salary of the employee with more dependents. The firm cannot increase the salary of the employee with no dependents. Such an action discriminates on the basis of marital or dependent status.

To fund the cost of dependents, the insurance provider increases the basic premium per employee covered. If the firm responds by reducing salaries for all workers, the employee with no dependents, likely to be more mobile, leaves. The firm cannot shift the cost of health care within the work force. Low-dependent employees are paid the value of their productivity. High-dependent employees are compensated more, because of health costs. The firm absorbs the loss, since it cannot discriminate against employees with dependents. With a publicly funded health insurance program, the employee is always paid on the basis of productivity, and the firm does not bear the costs of an employee with several dependents.

One way to reduce costs is not to cover dependents. The risk is that the firm loses productive employees, if they place a high value on health care. The paradox is that costs are imposed on the firm, and it cannot cross-subsidize across workers. It is forced to absorb some costs of employee benefits.

Offshore Production Location

In economic analysis, offshore location arises because of relative changes in technology, and prices of labor, materials, and equipment. Manufacturing processes and technology are standardized across the firm and industry. The method of production of a machine tool is constant, and often protected with a patent. Another location with cheaper labor cannot easily produce with relatively more labor. The production technology is given, requiring specific ratios of materials, labor, and equipment, and there is limited substitution.

With little substitution between materials, labor, and equipment, and a given technology, how are location decisions made? One can argue that exchange rates affect the decision to locate. If one U.S. dollar purchases more of a foreign currency, it is cheaper to produce overseas. This argument applies only if purchasing power parity fails. Purchasing power parity causes exchange rates to even out the costs of producing in alternative locations.

While one sector or firm might have a set of costs that survives a shift in exchange rates, it is likely that another would not. Exchange rates, lower costs of production, and technology are not sufficient causes of differences in production costs across locations.

The analysis is not confined to location across currency areas. It applies to location within a currency area, such as regions or states. Location decisions depend on externally imposed costs. A subsidy, or more favorable litigation or regulatory policy, is sufficient to generate differences in costs and prices. Firms can differ less in productivity, or output per direct unit of input, than in externally imposed costs.

Overhead Work Force

The work force outside of direct production has been increasing in U.S. firms. One firm notes that its most rapid employment growth has been in the legal department. Nonproduction, including administrative and clerical employees, has increased. Various explanations have been advanced for the relative decline in productivity of the U.S. economy subsequent to the first oil shock of 1973. They include lower educational standards, a shift in the demographic composition of employment, and an increase in the price of energy, which increases the cost of operating plant and equipment.

Accompanying reduced productivity growth has been an increase in the size of the service sector of the economy, producing other than physical goods. The increase in the size of the service sector, both inside and outside the firm, is partly the consequence of an increase in litigation and regulation. These employees do not always add to measured output of firms. A firm producing legal services by having to expend on litigation defense counts the expenditures as inputs, and not as output. An output of the firm is litigation services. The social benefit of regulatory compliance is not counted in output.

CONCLUDING REMARKS

Services, where no physical product is exchanged, account for more than two-thirds of U.S. gross national product. With the growth in services has come measurement problems. An economy has a slower growth rate if output is measured by input expenditures, with no allowance for inputs being used more efficiently.

Both legal and medical services expenditures have been increasing at rates faster than total output. The demand for legal services may have been induced by laws. Similarly, the demand for health services may be increased by medical capacity, third-party payment, and the low price facing the user. The G&A expense of the firm has increased. Firms have not always incurred these expenses willingly. They are not related to the productivity of a worker, or to the direct production of goods and services.

NOTES

1. Lee Iacocca, chairman, Chrysler Corporation, text of speech to the American Bar Association Annual Meeting, Opening Assembly, San Francisco, August 10, 1987, p. 1.

2. See M. P. Narayanan, "Managerial Incentives for Short-Term Results," *Journal of Finance* 42 (1985):1469–84. The manager has an incentive to develop projects with a short-term payoff because the reward paid is based on the short run, even though tenure with the firm is extended.

3 Tort Litigation and the Cost of Doing Business

Legal institutions organize markets, resolve disputes, and govern the conduct of business. There is relatively little analysis of the effect of legal institutions on business and its executives. In economic theory the executive is a passive combiner of labor and capital, maximizing profit according to specific optimizing rules. These rules are based on the legal structure of markets. In practice, dealing with legal institutions does not involve mechanical procedures. Some firms are better at working within a legal framework. They are more efficient at mandated production, even if less entrepreneurial. Economic theory views these legal mechanisms that regulate markets as exogenous. However, they impose costs, as firms comply with the requirements of the legal system. This chapter examines business aspects of the U.S. legal system.

There are two types of errors associated with the interaction of the legal system and the marketing of a product. One is the risk associated with side effects from the use of a product. Another is the risk of not being able to obtain the product. Respectively, these are Type I and Type II errors.

If the legal system is successful in rewarding a Type I error, the risk of a Type II error increases. There is an inherent disincentive for firms to carry out research and development. Those unable to obtain a product are usually not claimants. There is a reduced benefit to individuals using an existing product that becomes more expensive or unavailable.

In product liability, the Type I error is associated with the risk of

31

using a good or service. The Type II error is one of not having the product available. The DPT (diphtheria, pertussis or whooping cough, and tetanus) vaccine has been the subject of lawsuits, for harmful side effects. The increase in deaths from pertussis if the vaccine is not administered generates few lawsuits. Disabilities, even if not directly associated with the vaccine, generate suits. For the remaining users of the vaccine, the price is increased to cover litigation costs. Puritan-Bennett, a manufacturer of hospital equipment, no longer manufactures anesthesia gas machines.

More important is the effect of litigation on the operation of the firm. The firm spends resources, measured by its financial statements, in litigation. It cannot spend these resources on production. Its executives are distracted, and personally liable and named in lawsuits. These indirect costs of litigation do not appear on the financial statements. They appear in line items such as health care premiums. General Motors' largest intermediate expenditure, or vendor purchase, is its payment to Blue Cross, its principal health care provider. Liability insurance and legal fees increase the costs of health care and the cars General Motors supplies.

Aspects of civil litigation in the United States are discussed below. While the legal system is based on English common law in federal statute and in most states, the administration differs from other common law countries. Randomness and uncertainty have arisen in U.S. litigation and court systems. The randomness creates incentives for litigation.

ISSUES AND HYPOTHESES

The legal institutions of the United States have advantages. Products with extreme hazards to health and safety are deterred from being produced, or are withdrawn from the market. The product liability system forces firms to supply more care as a deterrent. Firms have incentives to invest in quality control and safety, with the standard set by the risk of litigation. Contingency fees provide access for low-income claimants, by permitting them to sell options to attorneys. Claimants retain freedom to contract, which is not available if they are required to fund all litigation themselves. At issue is whether these advantages could be secured at lower cost, and the inequity of treatment of similar claimants.

Costs are increased because of the requirement for liability insurance, the cost of litigation, and the cost of awards. These are direct costs of litigation. There are hidden, indirect costs of litigation. Firms that pay health expenses experience higher costs. The legal costs of malpractice enter health premiums. Malpractice suits increase the fees charged by physicians, and health insurance premiums.

The costs of legal cases have increased because of the complexity of litigation.[1] The complexity creates incentives for defendants to settle, given the level of future costs, even if a claim has limited merit. Access to the legal system is blocked for people with claims too expensive to litigate. The legal system is a mechanism for settling disputes between rich, or soon to be rich parties, but funded by taxpayers. The time and expense involved in resolving lawsuits reduce resources allocated to competing activities.

The Shift Toward Services

The composition of output in the United States has been shifting toward services and away from goods. Some of the shift may be externally imposed. The firm is mandated to purchase legal and other services. Some of the growth of the service sector is attributable to restrictions imposed by institutions. Because of this the economy produces more services and fewer goods, rather than because of legal mandates.

In 1950, $1.5 billion was spent on legal services. In 1950, of a gross national product of $288.3 billion, legal services represented 0.52 percent. In 1982, legal services expenditures were $27 billion, or 0.85 percent of a gross national product of $3,166 billion. The annual rate of growth for legal services expenditure is 9.0 percent for 1950–82, as compared with 7.5 percent for nominal gross national product. This expenditure is on direct legal services, and excludes the cost to the taxpayer of administering the system, the opportunity costs of time spent by litigants, and insurance.

Users of legal systems have constraints. There is limited substitutability for the services of licensed legal practitioners. Users cannot shift to offshore suppliers because of restriction on the practice of law. State bar exam and licensing requirements restrict mobility of attorneys within the United States. The restriction on the supply of legal services limits the degree to which the economy can substitute goods for services.

The technology of production is altered and constrained. A firm producing any good is also obliged to produce legal services output. It has no necessary comparative advantage in legal service production.

The level of legal services output depends on the hazard of the product, and the investment in its safety.

Level of Litigation

Since 1960 there has been in the United States an increase in the number of suits filed and tried in excess of the rate of population growth. The average award in cases affecting business, notably product liability and medical and professional malpractice, has increased at a rate greater than prices in general.

In addition to an increase in the mean, the variance of awards has risen. Across different types of cases, a consistent finding is that awards are increasingly concentrated among a few plaintiffs. With a few winners of large awards, and a large number winning zero or low awards, litigation has the characteristic of a lottery.[2] The lottery effect attracts more claims. There is a preference for a small number of larger awards. Increasing risk arises from the variance of awards. To guard against this risk, firms incur higher costs of insurance.

There is some evidence that the rate of growth of litigation has been reduced in the late 1980s, but from very rapid growth in the 1970s and early 1980s. The number of new claims under directors' and officers' and product liability have declined slightly. The award totals and averages have continued to increase at a rate much higher than overall prices, and the dispersion of the award distribution has increased.

Distortion in Intermediation—Transaction Costs

There are transaction costs in the legal system. Of each dollar spent on operating the tort liability system, between 30 and 50 cents is recovered net by plaintiffs. The tort system appears to be inefficient in delivery of compensation and services.

A study of asbestos claims indicates that of each dollar spent on litigation, 39 cents net is the compensation to the victim, 37 cents is spent on defense legal fees and expenses, and 24 cents represents fees and expenses of the plaintiff.[3] Values of the time spent by litigants are excluded. Such organizations as the American Federation of Labor–Congress of Industrial Organizations are in favor of reducing the transaction costs in litigation.

Inequity

The legal system serves as a redistributive function. Under the legal argument of cost spreading, a firm with higher liability costs increases the prices of its products. Buyers pay an insurance premium, giving them access to litigation should the product fail or cause an accident. The cost of the insurance premium is shifted between producer and consumer, depending on the price elasticity of demand for the product. The more elastic or responsive the demand in price, the greater the shift to consumers. A higher variance, and increased concentration of awards, increases inequality of income and wealth.

An increase in price because of the liability premium removes those willing to pay a lower price, possibly for less legal protection. The increased price is a tax on users, and less is demanded. If some products are removed from the market altogether, there is a total loss to the consumer.

There is inequality both in benefits, in awards made, and in the resulting price increases for goods and services. The price of birth deliveries increases because of litigation costs in health care premiums. Midwives account for only 2 percent of birth deliveries in the United States. Half of these deliveries are for babies of low-income women. Midwives are used extensively for deliveries among rural Southern black women. The annual malpractice insurance premium for a midwife, where allowed to practice, ranged in 1987 between $6,000 and $10,000, or between 20 and 33 percent of average income.[4] By comparison, the average malpractice insurance premium for a gynecologist or obstetrician is 10 percent of gross income. If the price of insurance increases everywhere, because of equal access to the courts, the relative price of practicing medicine in low-income areas increases. Prices of health care increase relatively for low-income women not covered by employer or public health plans.

Relatively wealthy women can afford medical care, or have a job where the employer provides it as part of a compensation package. If medical malpractice liability raises the fees of obstetricians and gynecologists, health care premiums increase. Firms cannot discriminate in hiring, but those hiring more women have a relative increase in costs of health plans. If the price is increased, consumers of the product share in the cost of liability, along with employees, the firm, and the government. The government bears part of the cost because firms pay medical costs from before-tax income, while employees do not include health benefits as taxable income. Employees bear part of the cost since medical benefits are included in compensation. The employer has the alternative of reducing direct salary if health costs increase.

Price Distortions

The transactions cost drives a wedge between the payer of the legal system's judgment costs and the recipient of the settlement. A distortion is caused between the price received by the payer and the recipient. For goods and services, prices are higher, but the expected net benefits of recipients are less than the price increases. This wedge creates distortions between the price charged by the buyer and that paid by the seller. The distortion in transactions costs prevents markets from functioning efficiently.[5]

Goods and services are offered in the market as packages including insurance protection. Suppose a firm makes a product whose price includes a cost of $3 per unit for expected insurance or self-insurance. The charges are for legal services sold with the product. Because of transactions costs, the dollar benefit to the consumer is $1 per unit. A risk-averse consumer pays the additional $3 in price for an expected value of $1 in legal benefits, a 200 percent risk premium. A risk-accepting consumer, knowing that the $1 in expected benefits arises from a diffused distribution, purchases risky goods or services as a lottery ticket.

The evidence of a minimum average cost of supplying a product of $3 per unit when the consumer receives $1 per unit in payout benefits need not eliminate purchase. Markets continue to function with the distortions, but at lower levels. If the average cost increases substantially, the product is withdrawn. If the price and quantity distortions are sufficiently large, a monopoly arises.

Another barrier to entry is posed by standards in regulation and litigation for new products that are not applied to existing products. The cost of these tighter standards is reflected in the prices of the products. A distortion arises in prices, with a fixed cost attached to each unit.

Quantity Distortions

The distortions do not apply only to prices. There are quantity distortions. First, the fixed cost of liability insurance acts as a tax on products, and makes all carry a bundle of insurance. This packaged bundle of insurance is a barrier to entry. Second, firms use screening and rationing in demand to reduce litigation claims.

The liability system acts as a barrier to entry for new producers, and in the limit creates monopolies. Such monopolies have arisen in the supply of measles and DPT vaccines. The system restricts a firm from offering a lower-priced product, given the fixed costs of insurance premiums or of self-insurance. The barrier to entry restricts competition. Smaller firms require additional capital to cover fixed insurance costs. The barrier to entry in new technologies protects existing technologies that may be less safe. The profits are shared between producers and successful litigants, as in a unionized monopoly industry.

The producer has an incentive to use rationing techniques to screen users and demand. There is a differential between the net cash benefit to the consumer and expected cost to the producer. The firm invests in technologies to reduce the differential. One technology consists of screening potentially litigious consumers. This screening consumes time and resources and is not socially productive, but it reduces risks. Another, more publicized technology is to increase the number of tests on products and services. Firms are forced into more defensive activity. Management occurs by rote rather than by a willingness to take risks.

Suppose a producer reduces the average cost of a product from $3 to $2 per unit, by offering less legal protection. The expected cost of litigation is reduced. This reduction is effectively unenforceable. The consumer cannot easily waive the right to sue. Waivers have an adverse selection, discouraging demand by less litigious users. There may exist a market for cheaper products offering less protection. Moral hazard prevents these markets from operation. Consumers buy the less expensive products, and avail themselves of legal remedies.

Consumers vary in the risk in the use of a product. Those using a lower standard of care are subsidized by those who use a higher standard. The driver who keeps a safe distance behind another is less likely, all else being equal, to have an accident than the driver who follows closely. If the automobile manufacturer identifies the safe driver, a lower price is charged. All drivers claim to be safe in their habits.

The litigation environment affects competitiveness. In final demand, all goods and services sold in the United States have the same legal environment. Production and corporate activity need not occur in the United States. Product liability costs affect the prices U.S. firms pay for machinery and equipment. Medical and professional malpractice affects the costs of health and accounting services. A price charged the user below the resource cost of the legal service leads to an overstatement of demand.

THE LITIGATION PROBLEM

Filings

Cost has increased with the quantity of litigation in the United States. The rate of growth of lawsuits over 1981–85 was 3.9 percent or 3.0 percent per capita.[6] Compensation per automobile claim increased 12 percent annually over the same period, and compensation in other torts 17 percent, as compared with a 7 percent increase in the Consumer Price Index.

The number of civil filings in state courts for all damage claims is listed in Table 3.1. Suits filed in federal courts are those in which the United States is plaintiff or defendant, where federal law applies in a locality, such as in Washington, D.C., or where the parties are from different states and the claim exceeds $10,000. In 1985 there were 866,000 tort suits filed in the United States. Of these, 827,000 were state and 39,000 federal cases.

Data compiled for 14 states with comparable information on tort filings are available for 1981–84, and reported in Table 3.2. In 10 of the 14 states, tort filings increased more rapidly than population growth. Total filings for all states in the sample increased by 4.66 percent, while the population grew by 1.69 percent. There was a 1 percent annual per capita increase in the number of tort filings.

At the federal level there were 117,320 civil cases filed in the U.S. district courts in 1975 and 273,670 filed in 1985, a compound annual growth rate of 8.5 percent. Some of the increase is attributable to a shift of litigation venue. Some case categories involving the federal government as plaintiff were shifted to federal district courts during the period. These cases include overpayment of veterans' benefits and delinquencies on student loans.

Table 3.1
State Case Filings. 1976–81 (millions)

1976	12.2	1979	14.0
1977	12.8	1980	14.6
1978	13.0	1981	14.8

Source: National Center for State Courts, State Court Caseload Statistics: Annual Report, 1981, Table 42, 58.

Table 3.2
Tort Filings and Population Growth, 1981–84

	% increase tort filings	% increase population
Alaska	13.78	6.32
California	6.23	1.90
Colorado	-6.21	2.13
Florida	8.38	2.53
Hawaii	3.15	1.93
Idaho	-0.29	1.26
Kansas	-3.71	0.69
Maine	2.86	0.67
Montana	1.21	1.16
North Dakota	2.15	1.25
Ohio	0.37	-0.15
Tennessee	-0.76	0.61
Texas	6.05	2.72
Washington	4.35	0.88
14 state average	4.66	1.69

Source: Kakalik and Pace (1986) Table 2.3. Court filing data from National Center for State Courts, *State Court Caseload Statistics, Annual Report*, Williamsburg, VA. Population data from *Statistical Abstract of the United States, 1986*, Washington, D.C.: U.S. Department of Commerce.

The increase in the quantity of litigation is more pronounced in certain subcategories, notably for product liability and medical malpractice. Data on product liability and medical malpractice filings are listed in Table 3.3. Product liability cases, usually filed in federal court if the plaintiff and defendant have different state 'citizenship', increased at an annual rate of 13.2 percent during 1979–85 and 9.5 percent for 1974–85. Medical malpractice cases increased at a 20 percent annual rate over 1974–85.

The U.S. Department of Justice reports that federal medical malpractice cases filed increased by 95 percent between 1976 and 1986, and by 192 percent over 1970–86, although there was a 7 percent decrease between 1985 and 1986.[7] Federal filings are only a small proportion of total malpractice cases. In 1980 there were 3.3 malpractice claims per 100 doctors in the United States, and in 1984, 8.4 per 100. In some high-claim areas, such as obstetrics and gynecology, 60 percent of those practicing have been sued at least once.[8]

The frequency and rate of growth of medical malpractice feeds into the cost of health insurance for business. It is estimated that 2 to 5 percent of the cost of health insurance represents medical malpractice

Table 3.3
Product Liability and Medical Malpractice Case Filings, 1974–85

	Year	Filings	Year	Filings	Period	Annual Growth
Product liability (federal court filings)	1974	1,579	1985	13,554	1974-85	19.5%
Product liability (federal court filings)	1979	6,132	1985	13,554	1979-85	13.2%
Medical malpractice (federal court filings)	1979	10,568	1983	23,545	1979-83	20.0%
Medical malpractice (filings as rate per 100 doctors)	1976	2.5	1984	16	1976-84	23.2%

Sources: Product liability: United States Department of Justice, Administrative Office of the United States Courts. Medical malpractice (federal filings): American Medical Association Special Task Force on Professional Liability and Insurance, *Professional Liability in the 80s*, November 1984. Medical malpractice (total filing): H. Manne, et al., *Medical Malpractice Guidebook*, Jacksonville, FL: Florida Medical Association, 1985.

liability. More than half of the cost of insurance arises in administering the system. Transaction costs of legal fees and expenses exceed payments to claimants.

Professional malpractice cases arise in legal and accounting services. The number of insurance carriers of malpractice liability for accountants declined from 12 in 1982 to 3 in 1987. Malpractice insurance rates increased by 200 percent in 1987. Arthur Andersen paid $137 million to settle one case. The cost of malpractice insurance accounts for 2 percent of total billings at the firm. Since the net margin of an accounting firm is about 8 percent, malpractice insurance accounts for 25 percent of the net margin.[9]

Regional differences in rates of litigation are indicated in Table 3.4. These data are reported for states with statistics consistent over years. The state in which one lives has a pronounced effect on litigation. In Florida the number of trials per 100,000 people increased from 89 in 1981 to 110 in 1985. The trial rate in Florida is more than double that in Idaho, the next highest state reported.

The risk of litigation varies with location. There is a variation across

Table 3.4
State Court Tort Filings

	1981 File	Trial	Rate	1984 File	Trial	Rate	1985 File	Trial	Rate
Hawaii district	1.0	44	4	0.7	22	2	0.7	23	2
Idaho district	1.7	386	40	1.7	429	43	2.0	442	44
New Jersey (auto torts only) superior	36.3	1765	24	41.7	1255	17	37.5	1225	16
Ohio (court of common pleas) pleas	21.2	1695	16	21.5	1955	18	24.8	2013	19
California[a] superior	81.0	3514	15	97.1	3817	15	112	3315	13
Florida[a] circuit	21.0	9049	89	26.8	11583	106	29.9	12540	110
Texas[a] district	21.2	1695	16	21.5	1955	18	24.8	2013	19

[a]Data on all trials were incomplete.
Note: Data are reported for all states where tort cases are separately and consistently identified. Rate is trials per 100,000 population. Court of filing is in parentheses. Filed cases are in thousands.
Source: National Center for State Courts, Williamsburg, VA.

states and jurisdictions, and an increase in the rate of litigation over time. Texas, with its elected judges and high campaign contributions, has been seen as a state with a legal system costly to business, as in the Texaco–Pennzoil dispute. Texas permits jury trials in a wide range of civil cases, including minor traffic offenses. The rate of litigation is increasing in Texas, but it lags substantially behind that in Florida.

The trial rate does not completely describe the problem. The majority of cases settle before trial. Case filings continue to increase rapidly. In California the number of cases filed was 80,970 in 1981 and 112,049 in 1985. The number of cases filed increased by 38 percent over the four years.

The rate of litigation, while showing signs of moderation in increase, notably in medical malpractice cases, is not decreasing in aggregate. The trial rate and the rate of cases filed are increasing. Where one lives appears to affect contact with the justice system. If the litigants and disputes are similar across states, the risk of litigation is not equitable.

Rates of litigation and trial are higher in Florida than in states where comparable data are reported.

A breakdown of specific tort filings confirms the variation in rates of litigation across states. Comparing ten large states in non-auto tort filings, California had a rate of 188 filings per 100,000 population in 1985, compared with 116 in Texas, 107 in New York, and 61 in New Jersey.

Awards

Since 1970 settlements and awards have been increasing at rates in excess of the rate of inflation. Decisions by juries are recorded, and data are more readily available. Data on jury awards for four types of common personal injuries are listed in Tables 3.5 and 3.6.

The source in Table 3.5 is the reporting firm Jury Verdict Research. The lower panel reports the nominal and real increases in median jury awards. Real increases are differences between nominal increases and the Consumer Price Index. If the premium is positive, the award increases at a rate greater than the rate of inflation.

The median jury award for a cervical strain injury increased by 12.7

Table 3.5
Jury Verdicts and Mean Awards in Personal Injury Cases

	Cervical Strain		Knee Injury		Vertebra Fracture		Wrongful Death	
	Cases	Awards	Cases	Awards	Cases	Awards	Cases	Awards
1980	145	8.4	102	43.1	46	78.9	93	466.3
1981	114	13.6	69	91.7	45	211.7[a]	121	758.6
1982	95	21.9	125	98.2	38	131.2	177	729.0
1983	180	19.9	156	100.0	93	174.7[a]	229	696.1
1984	152	14.6	136	128.3	87	114.8	215	587.3
1985	198	22.6	138	167.4	59	134.8	163	1094.0

[a]The mean is affected by a $2,000,000 jury award in 1981, and a $1,500,000 award in 1983 for vertebral fractures.
Note: Awards are in thousands of dollars. Wrongful deaths are for adult males.
Source: Jury Verdict Research, Injury Valuation, Solon, OH: Jury Verdict Research, Inc., 1987.

Table 3.6
Nominal and Real Growth in Median Jury Awards

	Cervical Strain		Knee Injury		Vertebra Fracture		Wrongful Death	
	(1)	(2)	(1)	(2)	(1)	(2)	(1)	(2)
1980	10.3	-3.2	7.5	-6.0	18.0	4.5	14.1	0.6
1981	15.3	4.9	23.1	12.7	17.4	7.0	16.3	5.9
1982	16.9	10.8	12.3	6.2	8.8	2.7	9.1	3.0
1983	8.7	5.5	10.8	7.5	14.8	11.6	9.8	6.6
1984	8.7	4.4	14.3	10.0	7.9	3.6	8.9	4.6
1985	12.7	9.1	11.8	8.2	11.1	7.5	16.8	13.5

(1) Nominal growth rate of median award.
(2) Real growth of awards over Consumer Price Index.
Source: Jury Verdict Research, *Injury Valuation*, Solon, OH: Jury Verdict Research, Inc., 1987.

percent in 1985 over 1984. The median award increased by 9.1 percent more than the rate of inflation. Since 1981 all categories of median awards have annually increased greater than the rate of inflation.

There is a self-selection in jury awards, where the observed decisions are not a random sample of all cases. The cost of litigating, in attorney fees and court costs, has increased more rapidly than the rate of inflation. Litigants are discouraged from pursuing relatively small claims. Courts and juries receive more substantial cases, leading to higher awards. While there is self-selection, the volume of claims has grown rapidly.

There are 2,564 verdicts exceeding $1 million. These claims can be broken down as follows:

	Number of Claims	%
Product liability	569	22.2
Medical malpractice	470	18.3
Work related	310	12.1
Motor vehicle	301	11.7
Professional malpractice	260	10.1

Professional malpractice includes claims against lawyers, accountants, architects, and engineers.

Data on the number of $1 million awards made by juries are listed in Table 3.7. The rate of growth of $1 million awards has been substantial, even if not adjusted for changes in the price level. There is double-digit growth of $1 million awards in every year since 1973. Since 1980 the smallest annual increase is 12.4 percent in 1985. In 1980 there were 134 awards of at least $1 million, and 488 in 1985. The average percentage growth rate of awards during the 1980s is larger than during the 1970s, despite lower rates of inflation. Inflation is less responsible for the proliferation of $1 million awards in the 1980s.

Studies of individual jury awards have been made by the Rand Cor-

Table 3.7
Million-Dollar Jury Awards in the United States, 1962–85

	Number of Awards	Percentage growth (after 1970 only)
1962	1	
1963	2	
1964	1	
1965	2	
1966	1	
1967	3	
1968	5	
1969	3	
1970	7	
1971	14	100
1972	23	49.6
1973	18	-24.5
1974	24	33.3
1975	27	12.5
1976	45	66.7
1977	70	55.6
1978	74	5.7
1979	109	47.3
1980	134	22.9
1981	250	86.6
1982	282	12.0
1983	371	31.6
1984	417	12.4
1985	488	17.0

Source: Jury Verdict Research, *Injury Valuation*, Solon, OH: Jury Verdict Research Inc., 1987.

poration Institute of Civil Justice. Awards in San Francisco County, California, and Cook County (Chicago) Illinois, have been compared. Data are weekly jury sheets of awards made. The data for San Francisco are based on 5,300 trials in the San Francisco Superior Court and the U.S. District Court of Northern California. In Cook County the sample comprises 6,000 cases in the Law Division of Cook County Circuit Court, and the U.S. District Court of Northern Illinois.

In Cook County the average jury verdict increased by 7 percent more than the Consumer Price Index, comparing 1980-84 and 1960-64.[10] The total number of jury awards has not grown markedly, but the number and size of largest awards has increased. The median award in San Francisco was $19,000 in 1960-64 and 1975-79, and $27,000 in 1970-74, in constant 1979 dollars. The relative decline in award levels in San Francisco is attributed to the adoption of tighter limits on litigation in California in 1975. There are increases in the real mean award in Chicago, with relative stability in San Francisco.

The variance and risk of awards is increasing. A higher proportion of total awards exceeds $1 million. There is a higher proportion of claimants receiving no award. In San Francisco, in constant 1979 dollars, the highest 10 percent of awards averaged $109,000 in 1960-64, but $236,000 in 1975-79. In constant dollars, million dollar cases are more frequent and larger. This trend at the individual case level is consistent with the aggregate data of Jury Verdict Research for the United States. Large cases account for a larger proportion of the total awards won by plaintiffs.

The shift of weight in the distribution toward high payments increases the risk associated with litigation. This increased risk requires an adjustment by litigants. The cost of insurance increases to protect against the risk. The distribution, with a small but increasing number of large awards, and a large number of small or zero awards, creates a lottery effect. The lottery effect attracts litigants. Research on the distribution of outcomes has shown that individuals prefer lotteries with lower probabilities of winning and high payoffs.

In an experiment on lotteries people were given a choice between a payoff of $5,000 at probability 0.001, or $1/10$ of 1 percent, and zero with probability .999, or 99.9 percent, and $5 with certainty. The expected value of the lottery is $0.001 \times \$5,000$, or $5, the same as the certain payment. Of sample respondents, 72 percent chose the lottery (Kahneman and Tversky 1979). A changed payoff to 0.0001, or $1/100$ of 1 percent and $50,000 payoff also has an expected value of $5, but is preferred to the lottery with $5,000 in payoff at 0.001. The prospect of a large award attracts litigants and more cases, even if ultimately there are fewer awards.

In addition to the increasing risk, because of the lottery effect jury verdicts are not equitable or consistent across locations. San Francisco juries give larger awards than those in Cook County. San Francisco plaintiffs won 59 percent of lawsuits that went to trial, with a median award of $21,000. In Cook County plaintiffs won 52 percent of the suits, with a median award of $15,000. In 75 percent of the cases, given the transaction costs of the civil justice system, in plaintiff and defendant fees and public costs, the parties would have been better off settling out of court.

The economic stakes are less than the combined costs of the trials, if taxpayer costs are included. Trials beneficial to litigants are not beneficial to society, if public costs are added. Part of the discrepancy in awards arises because San Francisco plaintiffs had higher claims on similar cases than those in Cook County. Cook County jurors heard fewer high-stakes cases, with two-thirds concerning motor vehicle accidents with minor injuries. San Francisco juries made awards that were 10 percent higher for work-related injuries, and twice as large in product liability cases. San Francisco plaintiffs won 54 percent of product liability cases, with a mean award of $137,000 in 1979 dollars. In Chicago plaintiffs won 40 percent of product liability cases.

The data provide further support for the increasing risk in the distribution of awards, with a greater portion in large awards. Decisions of at least $1 million accounted for 48 percent of the total of all awards won by plaintiffs in San Francisco, and 40 percent in Chicago. Jury awards have increased and become more concentrated.

There has been an increase in awards in specific litigation categories. Data on average medical malpractice and product liability awards are listed in Table 3.8. These categories are subject to occasional large awards. These awards increase the means in particular years. The increase in the mean award is largely attributable to a small number of large awards. In 1975 there were three medical malpractice awards and nine product liability awards exceeding $1 million. The respective totals in 1984 were 71 and 86. Deleting $1 million awards substantially reduces the overall rate of growth of total awards.[11] The data indicate that the litigation climate in the United States has become more risky, in that the distribution of awards for similar cases is more diffused.

The monetary composition of large awards differs from that of small awards. Noneconomic damages assume a large proportion of large

Table 3.8
Mean Jury Awards in Medical Malpractice and Product Liability Cases

Year	Medical Malpractice $	Product Liability $
1975	220,818	393,560
1976	192,344	366,081
1977	364,396	438,948
1978	419,372	1,687,187
1979	367,319	761,009
1980	484,726	563,438
1981	850,396	800,586
1982	962,250	850,670
1983	888,285	1,246,646
1984	666,123	1,021,986
1985	1,017,716	1,850,452

Source: Jury Verdict Research, *Injury Valuation*, Solon, OH: Jury Verdict Research, various issues.

awards, and are negligible in small awards. Noneconomic damages are awards made for other than the direct economic loss of the plaintiff. The two main categories of noneconomic damages are punitive damages and compensation for pain and suffering.

Punitive damages are awarded against a defendant as a punishment for unacceptable behavior in the delivery of a product or service. The rationale is that this will serve as a deterrent. Punitive damages permit some awards to be trebled, if the conduct of the defendant is proved to be willful and against a given statute. These punitive treble damages are awardable in various cases affecting business. The $3.7 billion award in favor of Pennzoil against Texaco in Texas state courts was trebled to $11.1 billion by punitive damages. Pennzoil accepted $3.8 billion to settle the case out of court. Punitive damages are awarded in cases for restraint of trade and wrongful dismissal, if bad faith is proved.

Pain and suffering damages cover the noneconomic losses in personal injury cases. The rationale is partly as a deterrent to future behavior of the defendant, but also to compensate the plaintiff for emotional losses. The plaintiff cannot be made whole, or restored to his or her previous position, under the legal doctrine of *restitutio in integrum*. The payment of pain and suffering damages compensates for this loss.

Punitive damage awards have increased more rapidly than prices in general. Noneconomic damages account for 27 percent of small awards, but 54 percent of large awards.[12] The average punitive damage award in Cook County between 1970 and 1974 was $63,000, but $489,000 in 1984, in constant 1984 dollars.[13] In personal injury cases there were five punitive damage awards by juries in Cook County between 1970 and 1974 averaging $40,000. In 1975–79 the average of six awards was $217,000, and in 1980–84, 23 awards averaging $1,152,000, in constant 1984 dollars.

Noneconomic damages are not subject to a uniform or objective standard. Punitive damages penalize for anticompetitive or other behavior. If so, punitive damage collection is more appropriate for a public agency as a fine. In the United States the plaintiff receives the punitive damages, in excess of the damage individually suffered. The damage suffered by the plaintiff is compensated in the economic damages. The noneconomic damages inflicted on society are paid to the plaintiff.

Costs of Litigation

Landes and Posner (1987) justify existing tort law and regulations on efficiency grounds. While the tort structure is not necessarily an efficient method of compensating victims or of spreading costs, it provides incentives to prevent accidents. The level of accidents is such that the cost of preventing them is greater than the cost of them happening.

This law and economics approach is concerned with the efficiency and not the equity aspects of the tort system. While courts redistribute income and wealth, that is an unintended consequence. Decisions of courts imply a standard of efficiency, by raising the penalty for failure to carry out a given policy.

A producer of machinery wanting to avoid lawsuits invests in quality control. A producer is more careful and invests in safety, given the risk of litigation. It is better to make these investments than face the alternatives of the legal system. The legal system acts as a deterrent, disciplining firms to increase safety and care. Economic objectives are efficiency, or production at minimum costs, and equity. Equity involves identical treatment by the courts of those in similar circumstances. With the tort system providing a penalty for failure to invest in safety, there is an efficiency investment by firms in preventing accidents. Contributory negligence as a legal standard is supported. Under contributory negligence, a victim is prevented from suing for an injury that he or she helped cause.[14]

The law and economics justification for the efficiency of tort litigation relies on high transactions costs in alternative dispute resolution. These transactions costs are avoided by tort litigation. Transaction costs for individuals include becoming informed about the risk of products and employment, of handling negotiations themselves, and of resolving issues.

No data are presented as to how efficient the courts are in delivering services. A court system need not be a low-cost information gatherer, and it uses police power to enforce decisions. The costs of legal system delivery have been analyzed.[15] The evidence does not suggest that the transactions cost of operating the legal system is low. The transactions costs, of paying fees to lawyers on both sides and operating the courts, and time in litigation, exceeds the net payout to award recipients. The transactions cost excludes the lost opportunities during litigation, and incompletely measures the time spent by corporate defendants in preparation.

The estimation of the cost of the legal system is based on two alternative data sources. One involves a survey of insurance companies. This survey is likely to understate total costs and awards. Some liability coverage is paid from policies not explicitly written to cover such awards. Product, malpractice, and automobile liability insurance are for an explicit purpose and included, but other liability categories are not insured directly.

The alternative, or lawsuit, method surveys court records on actual claims paid. The survey was carried out on civil cases by the University of Wisconsin Law School, in the Civil Litigation Research Project (CLRP). Projecting this survey overstates national costs for the legal system. Large awards are more likely to be reported. An accounting statement of the two alternatives is given in Table 3.9.

The total expenditure on the tort system covers the costs incurred by the plaintiff and defendant, litigation expenses, the time of litigants and insurers, and the costs of operating the courts. Excluded are the costs of worry and anxiety over litigation. The cost of changes in behavior because of litigation is not included, nor is the cost of the impact on future awards and settlement because of legal precedent.

The legal system, mostly in compensation for lawyers, consumes over half of the total paid by defendants to plaintiffs. The cost of tort litigation in the United States varied between $29 billion and $36 billion in 1985. Transactions costs involved in the delivery of these awards totalled $15.5 billion to $19.2 billion. The net recovery to plaintiffs varies between $13.5 billion and $16.8 billion. Other estimates of the transac-

Table 3.9
Total Costs of Operating the Tort System, United States, 1985 (billions of dollars)

	Insurance	Lawsuit
Total awards	29.8	36.0
Cost of litigation		
Defense		
Legal costs and expenses	4.7	5.7
Insurance cost values of time	0.8	0.8
Defendant values of time	2.5	3.5
Total defense costs	8.0	10.0
Plaintiff		
Legal costs and expenses	6.3	7.6
Plaintiff values of time	0.7	1.1
Total plaintiff costs	7.0	8.7
Court costs	0.5	0.5
Total transactions costs	15.5	19.2
Net awards to plaintiffs	13.5	16.8

Source: Kakalik and Pace (1986).

tion costs of the tort system are comparable, ranging from $9 billion to $27 billion.[16]

Tort cases amount to about 10 percent of all civil suits filed in the United States.[17] The plaintiff receives 56 percent of the total cost of administering the system, excluding the time costs of the litigants. Including the time costs of litigants, the plaintiff receives 46 percent of the total cost of the system. Transactions costs of operating the courts, paying legal fees on both sides, and the time of litigants consume the remaining 54 percent. The bulk of costs to the plaintiff arises in legal fees, usually on contingency where the attorney receives a portion of the recovery. Other costs, including fees to experts and court filing charges, are negligible by comparison, amounting to 3 percent of the costs to a plaintiff.

The cost of time of the plaintiff is estimated by two methods. In the first the highest wage in the plaintiff's household is used. Household wages are obtained in a survey of plaintiffs by the CLRP. In the second the minimum wage is used. The defendant frequently is an insurance company representing a corporation or individual. The CLRP interviewed the insurer as opposed to individual defendants. Executives and other employees of individual defendants other than insurers expend time on legal matters. The cost of the time of the defendant, other than the insurer, is not included in the calculations. Court costs include only the current salary of judges and court personnel. There are also employee benefits, including pensions and health care plans. Even with these excluded, average court costs were $535 per state filing and $1,948 per federal filing in 1985.

The bulk of the cost of administering the court system is borne by the taxpayer. In 1985 the total cost of operating the federal courts was $1 billion, but only 1.5 percent of this sum was raised from court filing fees. In California the average cost to the taxpayer of a civil suit exceeded $500 in 1985. This average cost includes claims involving no trial. If the case went to trial, the average cost for the court system alone was $8,327. The legal system imposes an indirect cost on jurors. Jury duty is required. The compulsion forces individuals to sacrifice activities with a greater opportunity cost while being present at trials.

The transactions costs are proportionately greater for tort cases, excluding motor vehicle accidents. For these cases the net compensation to the plaintiff is 43 percent of the total cost of the system. The defendant pays 18 percent of the total cost in legal fees. An additional 12 percent is the cost of time in litigation for the defendant. The plaintiff pays 20 percent of the total cost in legal fees and 4 percent in the cost of time. Claims processing of insurance companies and court costs, at 2 percent each, absorb the remainder of the cost.

Number of Lawyers

There is an increase in the number of suits filed, the mean and variance of the distribution of awards, and the transactions costs of the system. Associated with this growth is an increase in the number of lawyers. The number of lawyers in the United States has grown as follows:

1955	242,000
1985	620,000
1986	655,000

The annual average rate of growth of the number of lawyers for 1955–85 is 5.2 percent, and the increase for 1985–86 is 5.6 percent. The average annual compound growth of gross national product for the United States during 1955–85 is 3.0 percent.

The number of attorneys and caseload at the tort branch of the U.S. Department of Justice are, comparing 1975 and 1985:

	1975	1985
Attorneys	39	124
Caseload	4,000	11,000
Claims($b.)	1	200

The data are from the report of the Tort Policy Working Group, February 1986. The number of attorneys in the tort branch of the Justice Department has a growth rate of 10.5 percent annually, and the caseload grows by 10.1 percent annually. The increase in the tort branch law work force exceeds that for lawyers generally.

LITIGATION AND BUSINESS: PRODUCT MARKETS

Product Liability

Product liability suits affect manufacturers of goods. Under strict liability a manufacturer is liable for any accident arising from the use of a product. An alternative standard is comparative negligence, where the user is responsible for having helped cause an accident.

The justification for strict liability is that a firm spreads risks from a product by buying insurance. The cost of insurance is included in the price of the product. The firm has more resources than consumers in protecting against risks. The higher price spreads the risk among all users and the firm itself. When a consumer buys a product, insurance protection is included as part of a package. The more unresponsive or inelastic demand is to price, the greater the proportion of the price increase borne by consumers. The less price-inelastic the demand, the greater the proportion of the price increase borne by firms or suppliers.

For small aircraft the demand may be very elastic or responsive to price. Then the cost of insurance is more heavily borne by producers. For vaccines and pharmaceuticals, if the demand is inelastic in price, the cost and risk are shifted to users. If these users are not subsidized in price, the demand for vaccines decreases, and incidence of the disease increases. For infectious diseases there is an external cost imposed on society of increased exposure. Public subsidy of the price of the vaccine is not without problems. The subsidy is payable not for research and development, but for liability costs. There is pressure for increased compensation on a no fault basis, since the presence of a public insurer attracts claims.

A weak version of strict liability involves compensation solely for errors in manufacturing. An example is a defect in a specific automobile from an assembly line. A strong version of strict liability extends compensation to design defects and failure to warn consumers of problems. If the manufacturer is shown to have introduced a design defect, all goods sold in that class are eligible to benefit under the strict liability doctrine. Failure to warn applies when insufficient labels or other notification as to the risk are posted. Originally failure to warn applied only to construction defects, but there has been expansion to include notification against types of uses.

The expansion of product liability was determined by the U.S. Supreme Court in *Macpherson v. Buick Motor Company*. This case established liability on the part of a manufacturer even if the consumer did not deal directly. Here the buyer of a car transacted with a dealer, but liability arose with the manufacturer.

Risky products must jump a hurdle of fixed costs associated with liability insurance. Insurance premiums include fixed charges for basic coverage, with additional coverage declining in the price per dollar of insurance. For some risky products, a saving to society cannot be charged for in the price. The supplier bears the cost of litigation, imposed by the standards of society.

Three case studies of risky products are conducted: general aviation aircraft, sporting equipment, and pharmaceuticals. Since these are risky products, a high proportion of production costs are expected to be due to insurance. Data on these sectors indicate the extent to which these products have been affected by the litigation environment.

Pharmaceuticals

A vaccine has risks of side effects. The price of the vaccine includes expected losses from liability claims. The risk is spread between the producer and users. Society saves, by a reduction in medical costs of the persons not suffering the disease, and from the reduced contagion. Society, rather than the vaccine producer, receives the saving. Liability insurance is largely a fixed cost associated with the production of the vaccine. The marginal, or per unit dosage, cost of the vaccine is virtually zero, but the firm spreads the insurance charge across users. The demand for the vaccine is not unresponsive to price, so the firm cannot shift the entire insurance cost increase to the user.

The two conditions, a fixed cost and an inability to shift it fully to users, imply restricted entry to the industry, even without patent protection on the vaccine. The insurance premium is a barrier to entry, the cost of the vaccine cannot be recovered in the price, and firms withdraw from the industry.

In 1962 there were nine vaccine makers in the United States, but the number has been reduced to five. Of six original makers of measles vaccines, only one survives. There is a lower level of output and a higher price than with competitive supply. The induced monopoly creates distortions and inefficiency losses. With the monopoly the price to the user increases, particularly for those not subsidized in usage. The demand for vaccination decreases if the user price is increased, increasing the incidence of the disease the vaccine is attempting to cure. The firm cannot avoid the liability by moving production offshore, since the cost is associated with final demand and not with production.

Case Studies

Lederle – DPT Vaccine

The opportunity cost of not having a drug available is high, as for those not able to obtain the diphtheria, pertussis, and tetanus (DPT) vaccine. Where DPT vaccination is discontinued, albeit temporarily, as in Japan, there is an increase in deaths from whooping cough. The cost of taking the vaccine and having a side effect is a Type I error. If the vaccine is not taken, and the disease is suffered, there is a Type II error.

Type I victims have access to the courts, while Type II victims usually do not. Society places a relatively heavy weight on the costs of failure of a vaccine, making it less available. An additional problem is diagnosis error. A given illness is incorrectly attributed to the drug. There is usually an error-free diagnosis that a child has suffered from whooping cough, in the Type II error. The Type I error, where there are side effects attributable to the vaccine, is less clear. Under strict liability a child with a disease would be actionable against the producer.

Since 1984, only one U.S. manufacturer of DPT survives. Lederle has remained, after the exit of American Home Products. American Home Products was unable to purchase product liability insurance. The problem is side effects of the pertussis, or whooping cough, vaccine. Side effects are associated with brain damage and death. The legal system provides a punitive deterrent if a product causes injury from use, such as in DPT side effects. The error of not being able to obtain the vaccine is usually not considered. The monopoly, and increases in liability insurance costs, resulted in an increase in the price of the DPT vaccine, shown in Table 3.10. The price of the vaccine has increased tenfold. While a part of the increase covers risks for side effects, another part is the efficiency loss from reduced competition and production.

Lederle had more than 150 suits in its caseload backlog in 1988 against DPT side effects. One cannot argue that this number of suits is inappropriate. The level depends on collective preference. All recipients of the vaccine pay an insurance premium to Lederle for coverage against side effects. Some refuse to accept vaccination because of the price, increasing the spread of all three diseases. Society loses because of the monopolization of supply.

The demand for vaccination has declined because of existing saturation, and the reduced size of the cohort of children. A reduced demand need not create a monopoly unless there are fixed costs in the production of the vaccine. Research and development costs are fixed, and recovered from initial users. A vaccine in established use has recovered research costs. Fixed costs of litigation prevents the price from declining along a learning curve as more is produced.

The total value of claims against the DPT vaccine is 200 times the annual sales. The vaccine was first given universally to children in the

Table 3.10
Price of DPT Vaccine (per dosage)

Year	Price($)
1981	0.11
1985	2.80
1986	11.40

United States in 1946. Prior to its introduction 7,000 to 9,000 children per year died of whooping cough in the United States. In 1984 there were no reported deaths from whooping cough. This presents a large Type I error, if the vaccine were not to be administered. Because of a Type II error, a $7.5 million award was made against Wyeth from DPT side effects. It appears that the balance is shifting toward a higher price for vaccination, to compensate side effects. There is an increase in price and a decrease in availability.

Merrell Dow – Bendectin

Dow Chemical bought the pharmaceutical division of Richardson Merrell Company, creating a subsidiary, Merrell Dow Pharmaceuticals. Merrell Dow developed a drug, Bendectin, for use against morning sickness, which was marketed worldwide.

As with all drugs on the U.S. market, it was approved for use by the Food and Drug Administration (FDA). Once on the market, over 350 lawsuits were filed against Bendectin, claiming that it caused birth defects. Merrell Dow won dismissal of all cases going to court except four, and those were appealed. There remained a backlog of cases, with more being filed.

With the repeated backlog Merrell Dow examined the cost of maintaining the product. With no monopoly protection and no government subsidy as with vaccines, the demand was determined by the price charged to users. Bendectin was generating $20 million per year in revenues, with $18 million per year spent on legal and insurance costs alone. Merrell Dow removed the product from the market. The removal came despite the submission of a petition to the FDA signed by 12,000 doctors claiming the drug was effective against morning sickness. No claim against birth defects had been proved.

Precedent from one case does not affect another, because the parties, in the form of the plaintiff, differ. Collateral estoppel, or not having to repeat facts in various cases, does not apply when the parties are different. The defendant is obliged to use the same information in different cases, with attendant legal and transaction site costs. The removal of collateral estoppel need not solve the litigation problem. If collateral estoppel is absent, once a defendant loses a case, the implication is losses in all pending cases, and an attraction to file further cases.

The $18 million represents the direct expenditures on Bendectin. In addition, senior executives were repeatedly served with subpoenas to appear in the court cases.

Paul F. Orrefice, chairman and CEO of Merrell Dow, reports, "Our management, including myself, spends an enormous amount of time being deposed and appearing in court. I wasted more than 20 working days in 1986 alone on court cases."

Dow Chemical reported that its liability costs are substantially lower in overseas markets. Its dollar sales are divided approximately equally between the United States and overseas. In 1986 it reported $100 million in legal and insurance expenses in the United States, and only $20 million for comparable expenses outside the United States. It was defending 456 suits in the United States and only four outside.

Intrauterine Devices (IUDs):
Alza, A. H. Robins, Upjohn

Contraceptive manufacturers are vulnerable to suits for birth defects and wrongful births. The number of available contraceptive technologies, particularly for women, has been reduced. Among intrauterine devices, the Dalkon shield, made by A. H. Robins, and Lippe's loop have been withdrawn. Since 1985 there has been only one supplier of intrauterine devices for female birth control in the United States. The monopoly supplier is Alza Corporation, Palo Alto, California.

Syntex, the pioneer in birth control pills, is reducing its involvement. Alza, as a monopoly supplier, has imposed strict restrictions on distribution of its IUD. Women are required to sign an eight-page consent and release form prior to insertion of the IUD. The market is deliberately limited to 80,000 sales per year, and the price is $84 per unit in 1988. The high price is because of the monopoly and the inability to shift any risk of liability. With the monopoly Alza has moved backwards up its demand curve.

Condoms have been publicized as protection against sexually transmitted diseases, such as Acquired Immune Deficiency Syndrome (AIDS). However, prices of condoms have increased substantially. The cause appears to be a 1987 Atlanta appeal court confirmation of a $4.7 million award in a birth defects case against the manufacturer of a condom with a spermicide. Condoms carry a higher price to pay for potential liability cases.

The increase in litigation affects research and development. Reductions are difficult to quantify. Upjohn, a U.S. firm, is the manufacturer of the contraceptive Depo-Provera. While developed in the United

States, it was not sold there because of liability risk. By comparison, in France, research continues on a morning-after birth-control pill, and a once-a-month pill is on the market.

Consequences for the Pharmaceutical Industry

There is reduced competition in the supply of pharmaceuticals. This tendency is strengthened by a restriction in blanket liability coverage offered by insurance companies to drug firms. The liability range offered was reduced for most firms from $200 million to $400 million to $50 million. An advantage is created for relatively large firms, or those making less risky products. Since reduced coverage requires the firm to carry more self-insurance, smaller firms are less able to bear the risk of new product development. The regulatory and liability environment favors large firms in self-insurance. It favors large firms in requiring proven data on new products, leading to a longer research and development cycle that discourages smaller producers.

The liability and regulatory environment implies that drugs are available in Europe or Canada before the United States. The blood pressure reducing drug propranolol was available in Europe before the United States. The artificial sweetener aspartame, made by Searle, was available in Canada and Europe before the United States. Aspartame replaced saccharine, a sweetener shown to cause cancer in laboratory rats. An existing risk, even if potentially higher, is preferred to an unknown risk. A tradeoff is made between the risk of cancer with saccharine, and risks with aspartame.

General Aviation and Sporting Equipment

General aviation, or small aircraft, constitutes an industry severely affected by the costs of liability insurance.[18] In 1979 there were 18,000 piston or small aircraft produced in the United States. By 1988 the production had declined to less than 1,000 at an annual rate, or about a 90 percent decline in output.

The accident rate in the industry declined from 20.5 accidents per 100,000 flight hours in 1968 to 8.5 per 100,000 in 1985. Yet product liability awards increased from $46.6 million in 1982 to $210 million in 1986. The backlog, or overhang, of cases increased, even though production decreased substantially. The value of claims against Beech Aircraft was $447 million in 1984, but $1.1 billion in 1986.

The cost of liability insurance per aircraft was $70,000 in 1985, with Beech reporting $105,000. The proportion of the retail price in liability insurance for a Cessna ranged from 10 to 30 percent. In 1981 the manufacturers of football helmets received $20 million in revenue, and paid $16.8 million in awards and settlements. Single-engine light aircraft manufacturing in the United States has almost disappeared.

Since general aviation aircraft and sporting equipment are inherently risky, it is not unreasonable for a large portion of costs to represent insurance premiums. No particular percentage of costs in insurance need be considered high. The problem arises when, or if, the costs have been engendered by a level of litigation higher than is socially optimal.

These may be examples of unsafe products appropriately removed from the market by litigation. If there is a greater than socially optimal level of litigation, products disappear from markets where there is an underlying demand.

Services: Malpractice

Suppliers of services are defendants in cases for professional malpractice. Defendants in medical malpractice are doctors, other health care professionals, and hospitals. In certain specialties of medicine, such as obstetrics and gynecology, there are inherent risks. There is a risk of birth defects or other accidents in any delivery intervention. There are risks of taking no action. Death rates for both mother and child during pregnancy and delivery in the 1800s were high, and have been reduced. There are risks involved with any pregnancy. Unless strict liability applies, not all can be tied to the actions or nonactions of medical personnel and hospitals.

Suits arise against medical personnel and hospitals for malpractice. Hospitals, as firms, find an increase in the cost of doing business. Increases in malpractice insurance premiums are reflected in health care premiums.

The problem has been restricted in California following the passage of the Medical Injury Compensation Recovery Act (MICRA) of 1976. Under MICRA there is a limit on the nonpecuniary pain and suffering damages payable to a claimant in a medical malpractice case. The contingency fees for an attorney are restricted to maximum rates, on a sliding scale.

Professional malpractice cases are increasing in other areas, such as among lawyers, accountants, financial planners, architects, and other paper professionals. Since costs must be included in the fees charged, the costs of doing business are increased.

Patents

In high-technology firms research and development is a large portion of the total cost of bringing new products to market. The fixed cost of research and development is large relative to the variable unit cost of production. To obtain a return on research and development expenditures, a system of patents is required.

An intellectual property apparatus enforces patent protection. Patent disputes and claims of infringement lead to litigation between firms. The mechanism for resolving patent disputes is the court system. A small firm, with limited resources, is vulnerable in patent cases. A large firm can restrict the marketing of new products by filing patent infringement suits against smaller firms. This risk limits the capability of smaller firms to perform research and development.

Some software has been protected by copyright laws. Producers of software know that there is extensive copying, despite attempts at regulation. Copy protection results in inconvenience to the user. A site license prohibition, preventing copying within an organization, cannot be enforced. If a firm takes action to defend its copyright, it creates ill will among the user community. The consequence is that a firm must charge a higher price for the software, to cover research and development costs and losses from unauthorized copying. The higher price for the software induces further copying. Through the higher prices, embodying an expected amount of copying, some users subsidize others.

Directors' and Officers' Liability

A category of increasing claims against corporations lies in directors' and officers' (D&O) liability. Suits, principally by shareholders and employees, have been directed against management. Shareholder suits are almost inevitable in takeover cases, whether hostile or otherwise. The consequence of increased D&O suits has been a substantial increase in insurance premium rates, a reduction of coverage, or a shift to self-insurance. Firms are obliged to increase the fees paid to directors. There is a reluctance by individuals to serve on boards. Courts have imposed penalties on firms under the 1970 Racketeering Influenced and Corrupt Organizations (RICO) Act. This act provides for severe penalties on executives in liability cases.

One reason for the increase in D&O liability suits is the decline of the business judgment rule in court decisions. Under the business judgment rule, shareholders are prevented from suing to challenge decisions made in good faith. Two justifications underlie the business judgement rule. First, the courts cannot second-guess managers after the fact. Second, the disgruntled shareholder has options other than holding the stock, such as sale.

Court decisions are justified on grounds of cost spreading and deterrence. Cost spreading implies that the costs of a decision are borne by the consumers of the product through higher prices, and so are diffused. Deterrence makes the tort system a regulatory mechanism. High D&O liability insurance makes all products more expensive, and constructs a barrier to entry for new products. One case affecting D&O liability is *Smith v. Van Gorkom*. In 1980 Trans Union Corporation received a $50 per share takeover bid. The price offered was at a 50 percent premium above the market price at the time. The board of directors approved the takeover. The discussion at the board of directors' meeting occupied ten minutes. Only one written copy of the agreement was available, and it was not presented to the directors. The stockholders sued, arguing that the management should have held out for a higher offer. Trans Union was headquartered in Delaware, generally known for relatively favorable legislation toward the location of corporate headquarters.

The Delaware Supreme Court ruled in favor of the stockholders, holding the directors jointly and severally, or individually, liable for damages. The directors could have lost personal property in an award, but the case was settled out of court. The case caused the Delaware state legislature to enact legislation removing director or officer liability for actions made for "lack of due care." A more stringent standard of willful misconduct is required to hold an officer or shareholder personally liable. Once this statute was passed in June 1987, Delaware regained its attractiveness for corporate headquarters. Other states have passed similar legislation. If executives and managers are more at risk, they are less likely to take risks.

Competition

In product markets firms are defendants in competition cases. Litigation is a substitute for regulation. Less regulation implies more litigation. The prospect arises for firms to become plaintiffs in competition cases. In competition cases on trade issues, treble punitive damages can be levied.

Dumping occurs when a product is sold for a lower price in a foreign market than the cost of production in the home market. Another definition is that the selling price in a foreign market is below the price charged in the home market. Firms are defendants in product liability cases, where injuries have been suffered by users, usually individuals. Firms are plaintiffs against other firms in patent infringement cases. In dumping cases domestic firms are plaintiffs against foreign firms.

Financial Markets: Securities and Debt Litigation

Insider Trading

Litigation is associated with securities laws, which are largely federal in the United States. Securities laws restricting insider trading protect the public against exploitation by those who have more information. Research on insiders, as buyers or sellers, indicates that they are no more able to predict future movements in the price of a stock than is the rest of the market. Insiders are no more likely to sell prior to a price decline than the general public. Purchase or sale of securities by senior executives and directors must be publicly reported, and filed with the Securities and Exchange Commission. A waiting period of six months under Section 16B of the Securities Act is required on the sale of stock purchased through the exercise of options.

Senior executives and directors are compensated by being awarded call options on the stock. These options provide the right to purchase shares at a prespecified price below that prevailing in the market, by a given exercise date. These shares are either treasury securities, issued by the company, or purchased on the open market.

The executive pays cash at the exercise price. There is a 50 percent margin requirement, with half the purchase price in cash. To avoid taking out a loan to finance the purchase, the executive could sell a portion of the stock upon exercising the option. This action is not permitted, being a violation of insider trading laws.

The problem is more acute at start-up or venture capital firms. Here, the firm has limited cash resources. The compensation is in shares and options. To meet personal expenses the executive must sell shares or exercise options.

Class Actions

Some of the movement in a stock price is random. Suits are filed against directors and officers, and against the corporations directly, for unfavorable movements in stock prices, or for unsatisfactory delivery of products or services. Time is spent by the directors and officers at board meetings, and in giving depositions. If officers or directors have traded in the stock they can be personally named as defendants in lawsuits.

Rules of civil procedure provide for the payment of fees by the defendant to the attorneys for the plaintiff in class actions. Legal fees paid by the defendant to the attorneys for the plaintiff provide an incentive to litigate. Most members of the class receive nothing in a class action case. The transactions costs and the inability to communicate with those affected, reduce claims. Many claimants are ineligible. The firm is affected, in defending, in paying fees, and in determining who qualifies. The class action provides considerable leverage for the plaintiffs' attorneys, but on a one-sided basis. There is no risk of the defendant firm collecting fees from the attorneys for the plaintiff. The firm continues to charge the fees subject to the litigation, admits no liability, and pays attorneys to avoid further litigation.

The disparity between the high fees of class action lawyers relative to the low returns of plaintiffs lies in the compensation procedure. Legal fees for the plaintiff are paid by the defendant. As a reward for bringing high-risk litigation, attorneys are paid a multiple of their standard hourly rate. The multiplier is determined by the court, or as part of a settlement decision.

The multiplier in class actions ranges up to five times the standard billing rate. The incentive is created to bring class actions against large firms with deep pockets. Attorneys have an incentive to file suits, given the large fee returns. Plaintiffs have little incentive to collect the settlements. Firms are not deterred from continuing the behavior that led to the class action, such as in the insufficient funds check charge cases.

Case: Bank of America

In 1987 the Bank of America settled a class action case. The case was brought on behalf of an account holder charged $4 for a check returned because of insufficient funds. Bounced check class actions were brought against other California banks, including Wells Fargo. The bank agreed to set aside a $10 million loan fund dedicated to low-income housing, to provide $25 worth of services to each account holder, and to spend $2.5 million over ten years from the advertising budget on con-

sumer education. None of these expenditures represent any cash payment to the plaintiff deposit account holders. Over half the actual
claimants were disqualified. The only cash disbursement was to the
lawyers for the plaintiff, who received $1.4 million in legal fees and
$75,000 in court costs. The Bank of America was permitted to charge
for a returned check, and the fee was raised to $10.

There are perverse incentives in class actions. The plaintiff beneficiaries receive little compensation. The transactions costs, including
producing dated documentation, required to obtain a $6 refund on a
pair of Levi's jeans, of having eaten a Wendy's hamburger to receive a
coupon for purchase, or of receiving a no fee charge card for a year at
the Bank of America, are high.

Labor Markets: Wrongful Dismissal

Under Title VII of the 1968 Civil Rights Act, suits against employers
for labor market discrimination are permitted. The largest number are
filed by older workers, on grounds of age discrimination. Firms risk
litigation by any worker on the grounds of wrongful dismissal. Punitive
damages are awardable against an employer if bad faith is proved.

A wrongful dismissal award implies that a worker has a long-term
right to employment. A legal and theoretical notion is that of implied
or implicit contract. In the legal context an implicit contract can arise
if the employer has provided formal notice to retain the worker for the
long term. Formal notice includes welcoming letters and favorable
reviews. In the theoretical context, an implicit contract entails a long-
term association between firm and worker. The firm undertakes to
provide the worker with long-term employment, and to guard against
layoffs, in exchange for loyalty by the worker. If an implicit contract is
established, the employer is liable for compensating the employee over
an entire working life.

An implicit contract is difficult to prove. Litigation restricts the right
of the employer to adjust the level of employment. The labor market
ceases to be flexible if workers cannot be removed. The worker's side of
the implicit contract is unenforceable.

There are hidden costs of wrongful dismissal suits. Firms must
reprint and construct extensive employee manuals, instructing sup-
ervisors on the appropriate procedures for dealing with recalcitrant
workers. Firms keep unproductive workers, since the alternative is litigation. By increasing the cost of employing, firms are less willing to

hire risky workers. Risky workers are those with low levels of experience, or who have been out of the work force. Firms cannot explicitly discriminate on age, sex, or race in hiring. The use of experience or other characteristics correlated with these unalterable traits makes risky employees harder to hire. Firms are obliged to keep records on performance, maintain a paper and document trail, and inform an employee regularly of substandard performance prior to dismissal. Even if fired for criminal activity, an employee can bring a civil action for wrongful dismissal.

In the United States the typical pattern between employer and employee has been a spot arrangement. The employee who receives a higher offer at another firm leaves, taking the investment that the employer has made, and potentially company secrets and procedures. The employer is not able to recover human capital investments in training. Loyalty of employee to employer is not part of the arrangement.

Asymmetrically, when the employer severs the employee, the latter has recourse to the legal system. The expansion of wrongful dismissal suits in the United States is of recent origin. Part of the expansion is attributable to legislation, such as the 1978 Age Discrimination in Employment Act. Part of this is argued to be a redeployment of resources of plaintiffs' attorneys from medical malpractice. In medical malpractice, several states have limits on contingency fees and pain and suffering damages. Part of the expansion is the potential of collecting punitive damages.

If wrongful dismissal suits are part of the business landscape, the labor market relative to that in other nations becomes unfavorable. In Japan the lifetime tenure system is honored both ways. The employee who has received investments from the firms repays it with loyalty. This gift exchange, as termed by George Akerlof, implies that the employee remains with the firm, even in the face of higher outside offers.

There is a one-way loyalty. The culture places no penalty on termination by the employee. The legal system permits little recourse against an employee who has left a firm, even with training benefits and corporate secrets. The employer cannot terminate a worker without running the risk of litigation. The economic consequences in the long term are reductions in training investments and reluctance to hire. The targets of suits are large firms. The threat of litigation may explain the slow employment growth at large firms, as compared with smaller and medium-sized firms.

INCREASES IN LITIGATION

Several reasons have been advanced for the increase in litigation and the upward trend in tort cases.[19] Scientific advances permit inferences to be drawn on the cause of diseases not previously understood. This has led to retroactive strict liability. A defendant can be found liable for failure to warn of imperfections not known at the time of manufacture. A state-of-the-art defense is not always admissible. In *Beshada v. Johns Manville Corporation*, a New Jersey court awarded damages in an asbestos claim, even though the firm did not know the risks at the time of manufacture. The defense of retroactive strict liability is that it provides incentives for firms to invest in advance against potential hazards. The criticism is that an open-ended commitment emerges for the firm.

Other developments include joint and several liability, and the payment of damages before plaintiffs have suffered tangible harm. In another New Jersey case, *Ayers v. Jackson Township*, payments were made for medical monitoring and damage to the quality of life.

NOTES

1. See Selvin and Ebener (1984) *Managing the Unmanageable – A History of Civil Delay in the Los Angeles County Courts*. Legal costs rise because cases are becoming more complex, entailing more time and resources in discovery and deposition.

2. Evidence from state lotteries is that consumers prefer that the total stakes be concentrated in a few large prizes, rather than in many small prizes. The trend within the litigation system in the United States has been in this direction during the 1970s and 1980s.

3. Kakalik, Ebener, Felstiner, Haggstrom, and Shanley (1984). Defendants incur costs whether or not they prevail.

4. The discussion on midwives is from the Stanford Health Care Family Project, testimony to the California Assembly, sitting as a Committee as the Whole, March 1987.

5. The tort system efficiently allocates resources. This law and economics position school argues that the courts and tort system are markets, allocating resources efficiently. The effective function of the courts is not equity, or distribution of resources, but to induce the optimal provision of goods and services. The optimal provision of a level of safety in a product is induced by the deterrent of product liability awards.

6. See Kakalik and Pace (1986) as part of their analysis of the costs of the tort system in the United States.

7. United States Department of Justice (1987) *The Federal Justice System*.

8. H. Manne et al. (1985) *Medical Malpractice Policy Guidebook*, Jacksonville,

FL. Florida Medical Association. The guidebook contains survey information on case, claim, and award levels for medical malpractice.

9. The information on insurance carriers is from Thomas Campbell, testimony to the California State Assembly, Committee on the Judiciary, March 21, 1987. The data from Arthur Andersen & Company are obtained from the firm directly.

10. Peterson and Shanley (1983). An ongoing study has compared civil jury awards in San Francisco County (San Francisco) with Cook County (Chicago).

11. The United States Department of Justice, Tort Policy Working Group, in its March 1986 report calculated mean awards deleting those over $1 million. Including these, the increase in medical malpractice awards is 363 percent between 1975 and 1985, and 370 percent for product liability. Without $1 million awards, the increases are 26 percent and 87 percent, respectively. The medical malpractice increase is below the rate of inflation. A complete adjustment entails the subtraction of inflation-adjusted million dollar awards, since there was a high rate of inflation between 1975 and 1985.

12. Manne et al. (1985) analyzed malpractice awards up to 1985. The 27 percent portion for noneconomic damages affects awards up to $100,000, and the 54 percent share is for awards in excess of $600,000.

13. M. Peterson (1987) *Punitive Damages: Preliminary Empirical Findings*.

14. Contributory negligence is a part of tort legislation only in eight states, all in the South.

15. Kakalik and Pace (1986).

16. See Schotter and Ordover (1986).

17. The National Center for State Courts, *State Court Caseload Statistics, Annual Reports*, Williamsburg, VA: National Center for State Courts, various issues, indicate that in 1975 10.5 percent of all civil cases filed for torts, as were 9.0 percent in 1980 and 9.9 percent in 1984.

18. The statistics on general aviation and sporting equipment are from Thomas Campbell, testimony to the California State Assembly (see Note 9).

19. See Kenneth Abraham (1986) *Distributing Risk: Insurance, Legal Theory and Public Policy*, New Haven, CT: Yale University Press.

4 Tort Litigation and Alternatives

THE TORT LITIGATION SYSTEM

The basic characteristics of tort litigation in the United States are indicated in Table 4.1. One characteristic is jury trials in civil cases. Jury trials in most civil cases are characteristic of American, rather than English, common law. England has limited jury trials in civil matters. A size limit of six is frequently imposed, as opposed to the twelve common to the United States. Jury trials are not used in Japan.

The alternative, within a court trial system, is to have a judge make the decision and to follow precedent. A jury does not have full information or knowledge of legal precedent, and is swayed by immediate circumstances of the case. A jury trial with specific instructions from the judge on a range for damage awards, based on precedent, is an alternative.

A jury trial entails an opportunity cost of the time spent by the jurors. Jury duty is served under subpoena or police power by the court, and at a stated wage frequently below that in alternative employment. Jury service discharges a civic duty and contributes to equity.

While there is equity in the risk of jury duty, there is less equity in jury awards. Juries introduce randomness. Instead of equity and consistency in awards for similar claims, there is a variation. Some claimants are overcompensated, and others undercompensated. The randomness creates an incentive to employ a lawyer, for both the plaintiff and the defendant.

Table 4.1
Characteristics of the U.S. Tort Litigation System

   i. Jury trials in civil cases.
  ii. Filing fees negligible (courts provided by public funds)
 iii. Defendants:
     a. Pay lawyers by time worked.
     b. No cost redress against plaintiff for legal fees.
       Redress for court costs if trial award is below defendant settlement offer
     c. Liable for noneconomic damages (pain and suffering and punitive
       damages)
  iv. Plaintiffs:
     a. Pay lawyers on contingency fees.
     b. No cost redress against defendant for legal fees.
     c. No liability for noneconomic damages.

A court trial is a complicated procedure entailing the use of special-ized knowledge. While an individual is permitted self representation, a corporation must be represented by a lawyer in civil proceedings.

The distribution of awards is diffused, with a high variance and nonzero probabilities of high awards. This increased risk attracts litiga-tion, since there is a lottery-style payoff. There is an increased risk in the economy, requiring larger purchases of insurance by risk-averse individuals and corporations.

The tort litigation system has advantages. It provides a mechanism for firms to improve the quality and safety of products. With the ap-propriate incentives firms produce goods and services consistent with the desires of consumers. The firm producing a defective product suf-fers, with more liability claims. There is a market incentive to make goods more safely and to improve quality control in production. There is a deterrent to making unsafe or unhealthy products.

The mechanism is not free of government involvement. The govern-ment administers the court system, and the extent to which this activity should be subsidized is a matter of debate. The right of consumers to sue and collect damages enforces good behavior by firms.

Under the principle of deterrence society determines product safety through tort litigation. The producer who fails to meet the social stan-dard has higher insurance costs or spends more time in court. It is cheaper to invest in increased safety and product quality. The alterna-tive is increased litigation and exposure to tort liability. There is in-creased demand for a product with improved safety.

In an ideal world no government regulation of health and safety standard is required. The self-disciplining role of tort litigation forces firms to offer socially optimal levels. The difference between the consequences of litigation and regulation is that rewards or penalties are not received by the taxpayers but by private claimants.

It is unclear whether the tort system leads to an efficient allocation of resources. Inefficiency is suggested by the large transactions costs, and wedges are created between the cost to supplier and benefits evaluated by demander. At best, the efficiency argument obtains in output markets, and not in markets for financial services or for inputs and vendor supplies. A firm facing increased tort costs avoids them by taking production offshore.

The costs of doing business are specific to a location. By removing its headquarters to a state with less rigorous corporate laws, such as Delaware, or becoming private, a firm reduces risks of litigation. By moving its production offshore, the firm avoids the wrongful dismissal and termination lawsuits that make labor markets rigid and more inefficient. Once located offshore, the firm is able to export products to the U.S. market.

There are cost differentials. Domestic producers suffer litigation costs in employee and vendor disputes and in financial transactions. All suppliers sustain risks of product liability suits, usually filed in federal courts. If goods are more at risk of litigation than services, there is an incentive for production to become more service rather than goods intensive. While foreign exchange rates reduce the cost differential, they represent an across-the-board adjustment. They do not eliminate relative cost differentials, such as those engendered by tort litigation.

Contingency Fees

A characteristic of U.S. civil justice is contingency fees paid to the attorney for the plaintiff. Contingency fees share the risk of litigation between attorney and plaintiff. When there is no award, the attorney receives nothing. The attorney for the plaintiff receives a percentage of the award. This percentage is variable, given the freedom to contract between plaintiff and attorney. The United States is alone in having a contingency fee payable in all jurisdictions. Some jurisdictions in Canada, where civil law is administered by provincial statute, have contingency fees. Neither Japan nor Western European nations have contingency fees paid to lawyers.

Criticism of contingency fees has been directed at the propensity for increasing litigation.[1] Contingency fees give the right to the attorney to finance suits, and there is more litigation. Another criticism is that contingency fees are excessive, though what level is appropriate cannot be determined. An individual has the right to sell a claim, and so an excessive fee rate cannot be known in advance. Contingency fees present a conflict of interest, blocking settlement negotiations. An attorney for the plaintiff may have an interest inconsistent with that of the client. This problem arises from the ownership interest of the attorney. Polling data on voters indicate that restrictions on contingency fees would reduce litigation.[2]

The contingency fee system preserves the right to contract. The plaintiff is selling an option, or contingent claim, on the outcome of litigation. To the extent that such freedom is restricted, there is less litigation. The losers under the restriction are low-income plaintiffs.

If the United States is a defendant in a tort case, the Federal Tort Claims Act places restrictions on contingency fees. The maximum fee payable to an attorney is 20 percent of the award if the case is settled prior to the commencement of court action, and 25 percent otherwise. At least 18 states have placed restrictions on contingency fees in civil actions, notably in medical malpractice cases. In medical malpractice, New York, New Jersey, and California have sliding scales for contingency fees, with declining marginal recoveries for lawyers. Under the Fair Liability Act of 1987, in California the sliding scale is 33 1/3 percent on the first $100,000 awarded, 25 percent on the next $100,000 awarded, and 10 percent on the amount above $200,000, applicable to a wide class of claims. For medical malpractice, in California the Medical Injuries Compensation Recovery Act (MICRA) of 1976 sets a maximum contingency fee of 40 percent of the first $50,000, 33 1/3 percent of the next $50,000, 25 percent of the next $100,000, and 10 percent on the amount above $200,000.

The defense of contingency is that it preserves the freedom to contract. The plaintiff is selling an option on the claim to the lawyer, who becomes a collection agency. With a fully informed, risk-averse client, contingency fees produce the same levels of litigation as payment by the hour to an attorney. Such an analysis does not account for differences in access to the capital market to finance suits. If attorneys have better access to markets than plaintiffs, there are fewer restrictions against low-income clients when contingency fees are used.

TORT LITIGATION: ALTERNATIVE APPROACHES

Existing tort litigation involves transactions costs. The randomness in litigation, with a greater proportion of total awards concentrated among a few plaintiffs, increases risk. It is argued that the United States is developing an "imperial judiciary," where judges are making law.[3] Judges take cases and make decisions and awards in areas avoided by the executive and legislative branches for legitimate policy reasons. An objective is to deter frivolous litigation, defined as "totally and completely without merit" and "for the sole purpose of harassing an opposing party."

The tort system is not equitable, because of both transactions costs and the fixed costs of opening a file, even with low filing fees. For counsel, the cost of opening a file includes becoming familiar with a case, the opportunity costs of not spending time with more advanced claims, and the inability to substitute the time of other staff in meetings with the client.

The number of claims filed is restricted, because plaintiffs must overcome the barrier of fixed legal fees on relatively small claims. Defendants tend to overcompensate on small claims, to avoid publicity and litigation, and to conserve resources to contest large claims. Plaintiffs are overcompensated on small claims, once the barriers of filing costs have been hurdled.[4] Plaintiffs unable to surmount the fixed costs receive no compensation. A rational litigant compares the costs of pursuance of litigation against a settlement. Such comparisons lead to settlements in cases with limited merit, given the fixed costs of litigation and the inability of disputants to recover fees.

On larger claims, plaintiffs tend to be undercompensated. This is despite large claims accounting for the bulk of payments. Smaller claims are not pursued, or they are settled outside the court system. If a defendant pursues litigation vigorously and has more resources, a plaintiff accepts a lower settlement. If a defendant cannot recover costs of pursuing litigation, there is an incentive to settle earlier. Overcompensation to the plaintiff arises. Payments are higher than with no fixed costs of continuing litigation.

Equity across cases is compromised, particularly where settlements are made. Data on awards are the only ones readily available. They constitute a fraction of claims, since most cases are settled prior to trial.

With the lottery effect strengthened by restrictions on smaller cases, and courts not necessarily using precedent, there is a payoff to litigating. Any prospect of reducing the variance is appealing. Some lawyers are systematically able to improve the odds.

The risk of litigation affects resource allocation, by increasing insurance requirements, and restricting or eliminating compensation in risky industries. A barrier to entry is imposed by minimum insurance coverage. Alternative procedures for dispute resolution include no fault, workmen's compensation, no insurance products, regulation, and limits on litigation.

No Fault

A no fault system assumes that accidents are random. Attempting to determine liability is unproductive. A person involved in many accidents is unlikely to have experienced unfavorable randomness. This person is risky to the insurer, and has a higher insurance premium regardless of fault. A no fault tort system covering a wide range of accidents operates in New Zealand. No fault is applied in several states for motor vehicle accidents, which account for a large portion of tort cases.

In a no fault system, with accidents random, punishment and liability do not deter. No assessment of liability is required. If a party is injured, payment is automatically made. Each victim of an accident collects from his or her own insurer for wages and medical benefits, according to the policy limits. Pain and suffering and noneconomic damages are paid on a schedule. The consequence is a saving of legal proceedings. The reduction of the randomness in the settlement and award structure reduces the incentive to litigate. Transactions costs of legal fees are reduced.

Randomness is removed from the distribution of awards, with equity between plaintiffs who have suffered the same injury. No fault reduces the mean and variance of transactions costs. Mean transactions costs are reduced by the saving in legal fees. Under existing tort rules, awards may be increased to include payments to attorneys. Under no fault, gross awards can be reduced, but net awards to plaintiffs increased. The demand for litigation is reduced, because of the lower variance in the distribution of awards.

Inequity in awards generates the demand for litigation. The greater the inequity, the greater the return to reducing it. If there is no inequity, such as in no fault, a claimant cannot easily obtain a higher settlement by litigating.

The plaintiff benefits because transactions costs are saved, and more resources are allocated to awards and settlements. Defendants save the hidden costs of depositions, evidence, and the harassment of litigation.

No fault is criticized because the notion of deterrence, by punishing those responsible, is rejected. Under no fault a plaintiff receives compensation even when there is no party who is clearly liable. An incentive arises to include individuals and corporations with deep pockets as defendants.

No fault can increase litigation where liability is difficult to prove. A given percentage of births results in defects. The notion that someone should pay for these defects, even on a no fault basis, means suits against drugs taken before or during pregnancy. Since a defendant is argued to be able to shift the cost, liability deterrence and compensation are untied. Compensation is paid, but there is no deterrence. Cost spreading arises, since prices are increased to include insurance premiums.

Workmen's Compensation

Workmen's compensation for injuries suffered on the job is an alternative dispute resolution that bypasses the courts. In workmen's compensation legislation, employees waive their rights of access to the courts. For an on the job injury, victims are paid on a schedule, so there is equity between claimants.

Workmen's compensation of the no fault form evolved to protect firms against lawsuits by injured workers and large awards from sympathetic juries. In exchange for the reduction in access to the courts, employees are guaranteed compensation for injuries.

The characteristics of workmen's compensation are a fixed schedule of payments, denial of access to the court system, and no fault, or no determination of liability. One proposal is to increase the torts subject to workmen's compensation. A prime example is motor vehicle accidents, where a schedule of damage awards would be paid. The randomness that generates litigation is reduced. Japan has such a system for motor vehicle accidents. Total damages above a lump sum threshold are paid in stages, rather than immediately.

Under workmen's compensation, payment for an injury is known in advance, widely available, increased with inflation, adjusted to reflect social preferences, but not random across claimants. There is little market incentive to litigate. Minor motor vehicle accidents have been estimated to account for 90 percent of tort cases, so workmen's compensation in this area would reduce the court caseload.

Payments are made for medical costs, and a proportion of lost wages, depending on whether the employee is permanently or temporarily disabled and unable to work. The maximum benefit as a proportion of previous wages is set at a level below 100 percent, since benefits are exempt from income taxation. In California the benefit, or replacement ratio of previous earnings, is 2/3. The actual benefit paid is subject to a maximum weekly dollar amount. Pain and suffering damages are limited. The tradeoff for the limitation on nonpecuniary damages is the immediate payment of benefits, as opposed to determining fault and liability.

Workmen's compensation is efficient in delivery settlement to injured workers. Legal fees are saved, and the resources spent on litigation are reduced or eliminated. It is estimated that 65 percent of premiums paid for workmen's compensation by firms is received by workers as benefits. By comparison, only 42 percent of product liability insurance premiums is paid to claimants.[5] The differential is the transactions cost associated with litigation.

There are disadvantages of workmen's compensation. The system encourages a shift of litigation elsewhere. A worker injured on the job while using a machine cannot sue an employer under workmen's compensation. The worker can sue the manufacturer of the machine. Litigation is shifted from the firm to its vendors. Such suits need not be limited to goods. They are brought against suppliers of services, including software and professional services.

An injured worker is barred from suing an employer for an accident on the job. The employee is not barred from suing the manufacturer of work machinery, the builder of the plant, or the supplier of a good or service. Savings in workmen's compensation appear as costs elsewhere, in product liability lawsuits. The savings from workmen's compensation are overstated. Product liability suits are brought not only by ultimate consumers, but by other manufacturers. Another cost of workmen's compensation is the increase in demand by workers for regulation at the job site, including health and safety standards.

Workmen's compensation solutions have been advocated to reduce tort costs.[6] The randomness is reduced from the distribution of awards, and firms do not have to insure against this increased risk. In the cost-benefit calculation for the expansion of a workmen's compensation scheme, the benefits are the savings in transactions costs and lower premium rates. The costs are litigation elsewhere.

Market Solutions: No Insurance Products

An end run around the cost of liability insurance risks is provided by no insurance products.[7] A firm offers two types of goods. One includes full insurance against all risks. The other includes the same package without insurance. The buyer waives the right to sue, and accepts full responsibility for use of the product. The consumer chooses the level of risk, by selecting the insured or uninsured product.

Some consumers, not wanting to buy the insurance included with the product, are priced out of the market. Because the insurance is bundled with the product, consumers are obliged involuntarily to purchase protection. These consumers are willing to pay lower prices for higher risk, but are unable to unbundle the insurance from the product.

A similar argument applies to regulation or safety standards. A product need not be supplied with safety standards above the minimum required by public regulation. Consumers are offered goods and services with a choice of safety. No insurance offers a similar choice on litigation protection.

Consumers are offered a package of a product and insurance protection. A no insurance solution unbundles the two. By offering no insurance goods and services, the market for a product is expanded.

The major problem with no insurance products lies with voluntary surrender of the right to sue. This surrender is not legally enforceable. Moral hazard arises where a consumer buys a product claiming no intention to sue, but brings an action after an accident. On equity grounds, a user of the no insurance product is compensated on the same basis as the buyer of insurance, despite paying no premium.

There is evidence from other markets that no insurance is workable. The federal government does not provide flood disaster relief to property owners in high risk areas not buying insurance. This program is administered and enforced by a federal agency, the Federal Emergency Management Administration (FEMA), and subsidized by the taxpayer. A private firm is unable to enforce a no insurance provision. If high risk consumers do not buy insurance, an adverse selection arises. Those who should buy insurance do not purchase it.

When products are sold with insurance bundled, consumers are restricted, because there is no substitution between insurance and the product. Some consumers purchase more insurance than if a no insurance product were available. They must buy the insurance even if they prefer to self-insure, or have a different than average assessment of the risks.

Where no insurance products are available, buyers are unable to distinguish safety claims. All manufacturers signal the same quality, by making similar claims.[8] Consumers must become more informed as to which no insurance products are safer.

Regulation

Litigation and regulation are alternative interventions. One method of reducing litigation is to increase regulation. A regulatory standard presents enforcement problems. While a random sample of a product on average conforms to regulations, not all individual products conform. Enforcement resources are required, in inspection and regulatory compliance. Government regulations cannot foresee problems and costs associated with the use of a product. This issue is not resolved by tort litigation. A state-of-the-art defense is not always accepted by the courts. This defense argues that a product meets all existing production, technical, and safety standards at the time of production. Future developments could not have been anticipated.

Courts have difficulty in evaluating competing technical claims. As a solution, if a product meets a government standard, it has been argued that this is a sufficient defense. If courts appointed expert masters, or deferred to regulatory agencies, then a standard of evaluating evidence arises.

Under existing tort rules, both plaintiff and defendant present separate sides of a case. Courts determine the weight to be attached to evidence from expert witnesses. They are required to give equal consideration to testimony. In some cases opinions are expressed that are at odds with the prevailing body of scientific and technical knowledge.

Litigation Limits

Alternatives lie in restricting litigation directly. These restrictions include limits on certain parameters in litigation, for contingency fees, punitive damages, and lump-sum payouts. Contingency fee restrictions reduce malpractice litigation.[9] The analysis is counterfactual. Unrestricted and restricted contingency fee schedules are compared. The average settlement size in medical malpractice was reduced by 9 percent in 1976 using the contingency fee restriction proposed. The proportion of cases with no payment increased from 43 percent to 48 percent.

Contingency fee limits have been proposed for tort litigation. The Tort Policy Working Group proposed a schedule of 25 percent on the first $100,000, 20 percent on the next $100,000, 15 percent on the next $100,000, and 10 percent on the excess above $300,000.[10] Contingency fee restrictions limit litigation, but in a suboptimal manner.[11] Without contingency fees, poor plaintiffs are required to finance a higher proportion of litigation costs. They cannot sell the claim as an option to an attorney.

The U.S. Justice Department's Tort Policy Working Group has proposed a limit of $100,000 on nonpecuniary damages.[12] Both punitive damages and pain and suffering damages would be covered. In Canada there are no punitive damages, and pain and suffering damages are limited by the Supreme Court of Canada to $100,000 in accident cases. The limit was imposed in January 1978 in three cases, *Thornton*, *Andrews*, and *Teno*. Increases to reflect subsequent inflation are permitted. In California, commencing in 1976, noneconomic pain and suffering damages are limited to a maximum of $250,000 in medical malpractice cases. The application of damage limits to specific cases was challenged on constitutional equal protection grounds. The limit was upheld in 1985 by the California Supreme Court in *Fein v. Peninsula Medical Group*.

Total punitive damages payments in California for 1980–84 were $311 million.[13] The data are for awards only, excluding out of court settlements. Some states require punitive damages to be paid to the court, or to a public agency. Punitive damages, and their preponderance in large awards that dominate tort compensation, create incentives for a lottery within a lottery. There is a low probability of winning punitive damages, but a high payoff if successful.

Under most tort compensation, damages are paid as a lump sum, as of the date of accident. The lump sum is the present value of the lost wages and medical expenses, and noneconomic damages. An interest or discount rate is required to capitalize the lump sum. If different interest rates are used across cases, there is inequity in compensation. Annual payment of awards reduces the prospect of abuse and exploitation of a plaintiff, and reduces the tax obligations on the large interest income in early years.

Where the award for future wage loss and medical care is paid as a lump sum, the plaintiff receives an accelerated inheritance.[14] The risk with a severely injured plaintiff is of squandering an award, with the outside pressure received by any lottery winner. Had the accident not occurred, the plaintiff does not receive wages in a lump sum. The court determines the interest rate to capitalize the lump sum. If courts use different interest rates across cases, there is an inequitable treatment of those who have suffered losses.

The payment of awards on a staggered basis avoids the need for courts to compute interest rates, and makes periodic determinations of the medical care demands. One reason for lump sum awards is to permit attorneys for the plaintiff to subtract a contingency fee. A two part award facilitates such payments. One part, an initial lump sum, provides funds to pay contingency fees. Another part provides periodic compensation for lost wages and medical expenses.

Access Pricing: Court Filings and Statutes of Limitations

The cost of litigation is partially determined by the access price charged for the court system. If the price does not cover the average cost of operating the system, there is a public subsidy. A low access price increases the leverage in using litigation, as opposed to alternative dispute resolution.

The benefits of other government services accrue to the public, but those of courts largely accrue to the litigants. The government is operating a mediation service for certain types of disputes. There is discrimination against disputes that are restricted from the courts. A dispute between an employer and a union over wages must be resolved by a mechanism paid for by the disputants. Specific resolution methods in collective bargaining include negotiation, mediation, and arbitration. A dispute between an employer and employee over a job accident is handled by workmen's compensation.

Because access to the courts is inexpensive to litigants, case filings and trials become an early rather than last resort. Litigants are beneficiaries of the police power of the courts to impose monetary settlements. The cost of the system is spread across society, rather than being borne by litigants.

Charging user fees that more closely reflect court costs includes increasing filing fees, and a *per diem* court time charge. Another fee mechanism is for disputants to post a bond, in proportion to the amount at stake. Litigants are forced to use the courts as a mechanism of last resort.

Proposals have been advanced to shorten the statute of limitations on the filing of legal action. A time limit leads to a reduction in litigation, but less informed claimants are likely to lose their opportunity for compensation.

The cost of court filing affects the course of litigation. Filing fees should reflect the social benefit of public dispute resolution. Variable hourly fees are more efficient than fixed charges in encouraging allocation of court time.

Judges and Juries

For a party to prevail in a tort case, two questions must be answered. First, was the party injured? Second, was there a legal wrong? The determination of the two answers is placed in the hands of judges and juries.

A modification of the trial system is to have a single judge hear all aspects of a case, from pretrial motions to trial. With different judges time is wasted in repetition of evidence. Where attorneys are aware that the probability of having the same judge to hear future actions is low, there is little cost in delaying proceedings. The single-judge proposal presents scheduling and logical problems.

Jury duty is part of a command economy regulated and administered by the government. Individuals are required to serve, or develop excuses that involve the limits of ethical considerations. Society loses the opportunity cost of production of the jurors, and they are sequestered from family and friends. This cost is not taken into account by the litigants. If a decision inconsistent with precedent or prior expectations is rendered, an appeal can be launched by either private disputant. Society conscripts individuals to solve disputes between private parties. Where there is no jury, a trial decision is rendered by the judge alone. Society saves the time costs of jurors.

A philosophical argument for civic duty arises for jury trials in criminal cases. In civil cases involving private disputes, the argument for juries is less clear. A trial judge without juries does not eliminate the randomness in awards; a judge is not obliged to follow precedent.

A modified system obliges a judge to follow precedent. The following of precedent reduces the randomness and volatility of court decisions. Such a system presents a paradox. No need arises for either courts or judges.

Incentive Structures and Settlement

American Rule versus English Rule

The defendant, even if successful, is restricted from recovering legal fees and lost business opportunities from a plaintiff. This practice is the American Rule for free recovery. The defendant incurs a loss of time and opportunities. Reputation is at stake, and regardless of the outcome, the public perception of the defendant involves unfavorable publicity.

Under circumscribed conditions, a defendant can recover court costs from the plaintiff. Legal fees, the bulk of total defense costs, are usually unrecoverable. Recovery of legal costs by the defendant is possible only under malicious prosecution. The defendant must prove that malice was intended in the legal proceedings. Such intent is virtually impossible to establish. The consequence is that each party pays its own legal fees.

Under the English Rule legal fees are subject to judicial allocation. The court makes a determination of the prevailing and nonprevailing parties to litigation. An unsuccessful plaintiff carries the risk of paying all costs of the defendant. A plaintiff receiving a small award need not be determined to prevail. The nonprevailing party is responsible for the legal fees and court costs of the prevailing party. The English and American Rules are summarized in Table 4.2.

The rules differ for cases going to trial. For those cases settled prior to trial, each party is usually responsible for fees. The attorney paid with a contingency fee receives a payment on a preset schedule.

The American Rule has been criticized on the following basis.[15] The cost of filing a suit is low. With contingent fees to an attorney, the total cost to a plaintiff is low. The defendant is required to respond to the action, and incur unrecoverable legal costs. Even in a frivolous action or strike suite, the costs of continuing a defense create incentives for defendants to offer settlements.

The cost of litigation is the sum of filing and all legal fees, including those of the defendant. The losing plaintiff is not responsible for legal costs imposed on the defendant. The entrepreneurial risk of litigation is reduced, since the plaintiff carries no prospect of losses. The time and cost to defend a suit remain, even if the plaintiff loses the case.

Table 4.2
American and English Rules for Recoveries

American Rule

    Plaintiff

	Prevails	Does Not Prevail
	Reveives award	May receive award
	Pays attorney	No payment of legal fees
	from award	

    Defendant

	Prevails	Does Not Prevail
	May pay award	Pays award
	No recovery of	Pays own legal fees
	legal fees	

English Rule

    Plaintiff

	Prevails	Does Not Prevail
	Receives award	May receive award
	Receives own	Pays own and legal fees
	legal fees	of defendant

    Defendant

	Prevails	Does Not Prevail
	May pay award	Pays award
	Receives own	Pays own and legal fees
	legal fees and	of plaintiff
	court costs	

There are indirect costs. Litigation increases the degree of aversion to risk. Under Financial Accounting Standards Board (FASB) provisions in the United States, the firm may be obliged to report litigation on financial statements. Litigation affects the market value and borrowing capacity of the firm, even if it is successful in litigation. While there are penalties for bringing frivolous litigation, they are not enforced. Plaintiffs with limited assets are judgment-proof. Defendants gain little by pursuing a counterclaim.

Settlement offers and negotiations, while without prejudice, and containing no admission of liability, are interpreted negatively by the public. These costs of publicity are not compensated by the tort liability system.

There are circumstances where the plaintiff is required to pay the court costs of a defendant, but the plaintiff is never liable for the more substantial legal fees of the defendant. The American Rule is asymmetrical — the plaintiff collects legal fees from the defendant where there is no specific stipulation on fee shifting.[16] In class actions the legal fees of the plaintiff are recoverable from the defendant. The plaintiff must have acted for the "benefit to the general public or of a large class of persons." Legal fees are recoverable by the plaintiff from the defendant where lawyers for the plaintiff have acted as private attorneys-general.[17] Other cases of shifting of legal fees to the defendant include competition and employer discrimination.

Fee shifting applies after the receipt of a settlement offer from the defendant. The defendant offers to settle, and the plaintiff rejects the offer. The case goes to trial. The plaintiff fails to win as favorable a judgment as the offer. The plaintiff pays the defendant's court costs from the date of the settlement offer. The plaintiff can win the case and be obliged to pay court costs, if the award is less than the settlement offer. No legal fees are shiftable to the plaintiff from the defendant.

Exceptions to the prohibition of shifting of the defendant's legal costs exist in Alaska, Nevada, Oregon, and Washington. The remaining states and federal civil procedure follow the American Rule.[18] In Alaska a trial judge can shift defense legal fees to the plaintiff, but the amount is usually small. In Washington and Nevada defendants' legal fees are shiftable, but only in claims of less than $10,000. In Oregon there are many restrictions, and rules differ by type of case.

Twenty-nine states allow a shift of court costs, as opposed to legal fees, of the defendant to an unsuccessful plaintiff.* The remaining states have no provision for shifting of any costs.

The effect of the American Rule is to provide no internal disincentive to control costs. The defendant must respond to actions of the plaintiff, regardless of merit, and has no means of cost recovery. For the plaintiff there is a downside limit to the risk of legal proceedings. The lower bound of the payoff is zero, not negative. Legal proceedings differ from

*Alaska, Alabama, Arizona, Arkansas, California, Connecticut, Florida, Idaho, Iowa, Kansas, Kentucky, Maine, Mississippi, Missouri, Michigan, Nebraska, Nevada, New Mexico, New York, North Carolina, North Dakota, Ohio, Oklahoma, Rhode Island, South Dakota, Tennessee, Utah, Vermont, Wisconsin, Wyoming and the District of Columbia.

other entrepreneurial activity. While there is a risk of a zero payoff, there is a zero risk of losses. There are returns to a plaintiff with no cost, so a higher level of litigation results.

Modified English Rule

Under the English Rule (applied in England and its former colonies and in Japan) the defendant recovers costs against an unsuccessful plaintiff. Each party pays its own legal fees and other costs.

Under a modified English Rule there are settlement negotiations, and each party makes an offer. If the award is less than the offer of the defendant, the plaintiff has lost by prolonging the litigation. The plaintiff is responsible for paying costs, including attorney's fees, from the date of the settlement offer to the date of the trial. If the award is less than the offer of the plaintiff, the defendant has lost by prolonging the litigation. There is a cost associated with rejecting an offer for both parties.

Under the American Rule only imperfect capital markets act as a cost to the plaintiff for delaying. Imperfect capital markets prevent the plaintiff from borrowing the expected award. The plaintiff is paid prejudgment interest. The defendant is not responsible for paying the legal fees of the plaintiff. There is no additional penalty on the defendant for delaying. Defense attorneys, paid by the hour, have incentives to delay settlement.

Increasing the costs of delaying shifts incentives toward settlement. In one version of the modified English Rule, the plaintiff claims $100,000 and rejects a defendant's offer of $75,000. If the court awards the $100,000, the defendant pays legal fees for both sides. If the award is $50,000, the plaintiff pays two sets of fees, for a better result could have been obtained by settling.

In another variant the fee shifting is based on the difference between the award and the rejected offer — the closer the difference, the smaller the fee shift; the wider the difference, the greater the penalty on the party called on to pay. In the above example, if the defendant's offer is $75,000, the award is 33⅓ percent higher than the offer. The defendant could be required to pay 33⅓ percent of the fees of the plaintiff. If the award is $50,000 (or 33⅓ percent lower), the plaintiff is required to pay 33⅓ percent of the fees of the defendant. Going to court results in a potential liability for the marginal costs of attorney and other fees. By increasing the price of going to court, litigation is reduced. If a party has rejected an offer, it has imposed on the courts and is penalized.

A lower level of litigation in England than in the United States need not be solely because of the English Rule. A court may make larger awards. These awards cover the risk to the plaintiff of having to pay legal fees. When the courts pay no regard to fee-shifting rules in awards, the English Rule reduces less meritorious cases.

All else being equal, under the American Rule awards are lower, since there is no risk of legal fees awarded against the plaintiff. Judges, and lawyers in negotiations, are aware that plaintiffs' attorneys are paid on a contingency. They know that defendants' lawyers are never paid by the plaintiff. If there is a risk of a plaintiff paying the fees of a defendant in an unsuccessful action, an award is made to compensate. Total awards are higher, to compensate on average for those plaintiffs required to pay defendants' costs. If American awards have been grossed up to include attorney's fees, the English Rule reduces awards. Otherwise, the defendant is liable for the award and legal fees of a successful plaintiff. The quantity of litigation, as the number of suits filed, need not be reduced. The discouragement of filing relatively small claims is removed.

More litigation arises from smaller suits. A system with fixed costs of filing results in a reluctance to litigate small matters. Under the American Rule a person with a $5,000 claim is discouraged from litigation. Even if successful, the plaintiff pays filing fees and a contingency to the attorney. A successful plaintiff under the English Rule asks for recovery of legal fees.

A judgment against a plaintiff for costs may not be satisfied, and causes problems of collection. The problem of the impecunious plaintiff can be solved by a levy imposed by the courts. Higher filing fees have a discouraging effect on the poor. The shift of the litigation risk to plaintiffs and their attorneys reduces litigation. Risk-free or risk-reduced litigation is argued to have social benefit.[19]

The English Rule has administrative costs of determining legal fees. The repayment to a successful plaintiff of the fees for an attorney must be reasonable. This reasonableness requires the court to impose a schedule of contingency fees, involving more regulation of matters between attorney and client. Regulated contingency fees, a fund to reward successful defendants, and the recording in court of offers are required.

Polling data of California voters, on whether a losing plaintiff should pay the legal fees of a winning defendant, indicate support by 46 percent to 41 percent.[20] The respondents were told that in other industrial nations, including the United Kingdom and Japan, the losing plaintiff is required to pay legal fees. With this information the polling data favored the English Rule by 45 percent to 30 percent. The respondents were told that under the English Rule some low- or middle-income litigants might pay the costs of high-income defendants. The response reversed to 23 percent in favor to 65 percent opposed.

It has been argued that an English Rule eases court congestion and provides incentives for the plaintiffs to settle.[21] The barrier to entry of small claimants is removed, with the prospect of recovering legal fees. The actual recovery is not reduced, as with contingency fees. With strong cases for small amounts, plaintiffs receive settlements where existing litigation prevents recovery.[22] Lawyers for the plaintiff take entrepreneurial risks, by buying options from the claimant. The risk is more complete by providing for potential losses if there is no recovery. It is possible that call and put options could be made available. There is no reason for more active markets to develop, where insurance companies or other investors buy and sell options on cases from litigants and their attorneys.

Court Procedures

Joint and Several Liability

Joint and several liability involves the option of the plaintiff to collect from any defendant, regardless of the allocation of liability. This deep pockets provision creates an incentive to add large corporations and governments and wealthy individuals as defendants in liability cases. If such defendants are found to be 1 percent liable, they can be asked to pay all damage awards.

In California Proposition 51, passed by voters in June 1986, provides that in noneconomic pain and suffering awards a defendant is only liable proportionately, and not for the entire claim. A defendant 1 percent liable pays 1 percent of noneconomic damages, the largest component of large awards.

Strict Liability

Under strict liability an injury resulting from a use of a product is actionable and compensable. Compensation arises from broader uses of products. In California the Fair Settlement Act of 1987 provides that in product liability cases, punitive damages can be awarded only under certain conditions, as a modification of strict liability. The plaintiff must prove that the action of the producer was "despicable." Court cases are required to define despicable behavior. There must be responsible use. If a product is inherently dangerous, the producer is not necessarily liable. "Clear and convincing evidence" of liability must be presented. Volunteers in nonprofit organizations are protected against suits.

Capacity of Legal Services

The United States has a large supply of lawyers, with little prospect of a reduction in the growth of entry to the profession. As many lawyers enter the profession in the United States each year as the total in Japan.

Three hypotheses are suggested as to why an increase in the number of attorneys is likely to lead to increases in the per capita level of litigation: disequilibrium, market demand, and supply-driven demand. The disequilibrium hypothesis holds that the price to users of legal services is restrained below the equilibrium level. There is an excess demand at the observed market price. The price paid by the user is not the full cost of the service. Part of the cost is the imposition on court facilities, paid for by a third party, the government, and part is imposed on the other disputant. Because the price charged the user is below the average cost imposed, an excess demand arises. The excess demand is strengthened by contingency fees that shift the risk from litigant to attorney. An increase in the supply of lawyers does not reduce the price of the service. Since the market is supply constrained, the amount of litigation is increased, with no reduction in price. There is a perpetual excess demand.

The second hypothesis is based on market demand. An increase in the number of attorneys reduces the cost of using one, even if fees are not reduced. The indirect costs of search and transit time for users is reduced, as the service is more densely available. The price to the user is the sum of out-of-pocket costs and the opportunity cost of time. The time opportunity cost is relatively the larger, so there is a reduction in the price of legal services to the user, resulting in an increase in demand.

The third hypothesis is that attorneys are able to develop demand for the product. Similar arguments apply to medical care. Medical practitioners are specialized, and have more information on medical diagnosis than do patients.[23] There is asymmetric information, in that the attorney is more familiar with legal procedures than is the client. The incentive is to suggest more intervention.

Lawyers are not charging clients the full cost of litigation. The cost of court services and the costs imposed on defendants are excluded from charges levied on the client. The increase in the supply of lawyers increases competition, and reduces the direct cost, such as in lower contingency fee rates, or hiring a lawyer. The cost to the litigant is reduced, while the total cost of tort actions increases. The consequence is more litigation, increasing the demand for lawyers.

Medical data have direct output measures, such as infant mortality and life. In legal services output measures are more nebulous. If the exercise of rights is measured as output, legal service input and output are identical. On these input measures, the United States has higher rates of litigation than competitors in world markets such as Japan and West Germany.

If increased capacity raises litigation and costs above a socially acceptable level, a policy measure is to reduce supply. Costs of becoming a medical practitioner include the foregone earnings of the student, and the cost of providing medical schools and facilities. The latter facilities are expensive. For new law school graduates, investment costs are relatively low. Large investments in educational institutions are not required. The low investment facilitates part-time study, where the student can take courses with no loss in foregone income. To raise the price of entry, the most feasible procedure is to make it more difficult to pass the bar examination. Another possibility is to increase filing fees for court usage.

Alternative Dispute Resolution

There is a bias in the United States toward court procedures, and disputes involving lawyers. Attorneys for plaintiffs are paid on a contingency. Awards and settlements are increased by prejudgment interest at a rate in excess of the rate of inflation. Estimates of this prejudgment interest rate of 3.7 percent above the rate of inflation have been obtained.[24] While plaintiffs are not necessarily able to borrow against these delayed settlements, they are compensated for delays.

There is little incentive to settle disputes immediately. The incentives are perverse for defense attorneys. There is a meter ticking incentive. The longer that the defense attorney, whether retained as outside counsel or as an inside corporate attorney, delays, the larger is the total fee. Neither attorney has an incentive to settle early, except at the court-house door, to avoid the risk of an imposed settlement.

The defendant saves legal costs by making an immediate settlement offer at an amount awarded in a comparable case. Such a strategy applies in motor vehicle accidents or in other torts where there is a large body of case law and precedent. In tort areas with limited prece-dent, there is less basis to offer an immediate settlement.

There is a psychological effect on defendants. Possibly encouraged by defense counsel, but also exogenously, there is a tendency to resist and fight all charges. This reaction is irrational in that the costs of paying immediately are less than those of delaying.

Prospect theory argues that individuals, and possibly corporations, behave in a loss-avoidance manner.[25] Consider a choice between a small loss with certainty and a lottery with alternatives of no loss or a large loss. Decision makers overwhelmingly prefer the lottery, even when its expected value is lower than the certainty equivalent.

Suppose a defendant has the prospect of accepting a settlement pro-posal for $20,000 immediately. The alternative is continuation of liti-gation, including a trial where the outcome is uncertain. In the trial, the defendant has a 20 percent probability of paying no award, but an 80 percent probability of paying $25,000. The prospects are:

Certainty equivalent $20,000
Expected value $20,000 = $0 × 0.2 + $25,000 × 0.8

The first situation involves no risk. Court and legal costs of the trial are zero. A risk-averse defendant prefers to pay the $20,000. If the proba-bility of the award were $30,000 at trial, the options are:

Certainty equivalent $20,000
Expected value $24,000 = $0 × 0.2 + $30,000 × 0.8

In the latter case the defendant has a choice between paying $20,000 with certainty, or taking a chance on paying nothing or $30,000. Even though the expected outcome of a $24,000 payout exceeds the $20,000 as a loss to the firm, the firm gambles on continuing litigation. This incentive to gamble continues either up to trial and appeals, or creates a delay in settlement.

The choices facing the defendant are a $20,000 payout with certain-ty and a lottery with an expected payout of $24,000. While these sums are sufficiently low that swift settlement is almost certain, consider alternatives in compensating the defense attorney. The attorney is paid $2,000 in fees for the settlement option, or $5,000 in costs if litigation continues.

Total expected costs for the firm as defendant are:

Certainty equivalent (accept settlement now) $20,000+$2,000=$22,000

Expected value (delay) $24,000+$5,000=$29,000

Since the defendant has a preference for risk, there remains a tendency to delay, though less so than before, since legal costs are included. The expert, the defense attorney, to whom the client defers, has the same incentive.

If the defendant values the case at $24,000 and pays a contingency fee of 25 percent, the defense attorney receives:

Settle immediately $2,000

Continue $0.25 \times \$24,000 = \$6,000$

If the zero award is made, the attorney receives 25 percent of $24,000 less zero. If the award of $30,000 is made, the attorney receives nothing. The expected fee is $6,000, as compared with $5,000 on the time-billed basis. As in construction or in public cost-plus contracting, a time basis leads to no incentive to reduce costs.

The attorney is compensated for risk, being paid $6,000 versus $5,000. The contingency payment is a function of the difference between the actual award or settlement and the target. The attorney, if not having the choice of the 'time and materials' option, is more likely to promote a settlement, bearing a risk of the litigation. Under the existing asymmetry, the attorney for the plaintiff is an entrepreneur, while the attorney for the defendant is not.

Prospect theory argues that those facing losses (defendants) have an incentive to gamble. Those facing gains (plaintiffs) have an incentive to be risk averse, and to accept settlements. Plaintiffs have two incentives to delay. One is the prejudgment interest, which is compensation for the risk of delay. The other is the money's worth incentive of attorneys for the plaintiff.

When there is a positive expected value of payoff, as for plaintiffs, decision makers are risk averse. Their valuation of the benefit of the award increases with the payoff at a decreasing rate. Where the expected payoff is negative, as for defendants, decision makers are risk accepting. Their valuation of the cost of the award decreases at a decreasing rate with the loss suffered. Strengthening the argument is the willingness to accept risk increases with wealth, since defendants are usually more wealthy than plaintiffs.

Defendants have an incentive to prolong litigation. Plaintiffs usually have an incentive to shorten it. Defendants are more likely to request postponements and adjournments, as tactical measures to cudgel plaintiffs into a settlement, and to take advantage of risk attitudes.

Even if both litigants are risk averse, but defendants less so by virtue of wealth, the defendant retains an incentive to delay. A delay increases the prospect of settlement by the plaintiff. Prospect theory provides a rationale for gambling by the defendant. Capital markets are imperfect, and plaintiffs are unable to borrow fully against an expected award. With awards uncertain, financial institutions discount expected awards in loans to plaintiffs.

Compensation of lawyers in the United States is asymmetrical. The lawyer for the plaintiff is paid on contingency, and that for the defendant paid by the hour.

Defense attorneys have more incentive to settle if paid on a contingency. Delaying, seeking more depositions, and expanding the discovery process are then cost rather than revenue items for defense counsel. Pretrial motions and delays have low or no penalties in the court system.

In a contingent fee scheme for the defense attorney, the defendant makes a settlement offer. If this offer is rejected, the case goes to trial. The defense attorney is paid on the basis of the difference between the award and settlement. Since the attorney is being paid on the basis of productivity to the client, rather than on input, there is an incentive to reduce the time spent in litigation. Under existing procedures, a delay in proceeding holds the plaintiff harmless (since prejudgment interest is paid) increases the cost to the defendant, and increases defense attorney fees.

There are opportunity costs of time and resources. Incentive perversities arise in restrictions on contingency fees. In legislative restrictions on fees, the retention rate by the attorney per dollar collected decreases with the size of the award. For example, while the attorney collects 40 cents on the first dollar, on a dollar over $200,000 the attorney is limited to 10 cents by statute.

The attorney has a low recovery from pursuing additional litigation, and an incentive to accept a lower offer than otherwise. Time can be allocated to another case with a higher marginal return. On one case the attorney stands to gain only 10 cents by obtaining another dollar for the client, while the alternative is 40 cents on another case.

If 40 cents is the standard recovery rate, 10 cents is restricted below that prevailing in the market, the attorney for the plaintiff has an incentive to allocate time to other cases. The plaintiff is restricted from the ability to contract. Any reduction in litigation is at the expense of the plaintiff. Unable to shift the risk, the plaintiff either absorbs the costs or limits litigation. The limitation of litigation arises not so much on efficiency grounds as on a tax imposed on a plaintiff entitled to a large award.

Collateral Offset

Receipts from collateral sources, such as an insurance policy, workmen's compensation, disability plan, or unemployment benefits, are not always subtracted from the settlement. A person receives double compensation for the same accident.

Collateral offset provisions are typically included in tort reform, including that proposed by the Tort Policy Working Group of the U.S. Justice Department.[26] The only restriction is on subrogation. The payer of an award, such as an insurance company, retains the right to collect from the defendant in a seperate action.

There is a moral hazard with collateral offset. The person who has collateral insurance, such as a disability plan, has paid a premium for coverage against the risk of an accident. The premium payment is a cost for the employee, or is part of a compensation package with an employer. The person who has no insurance has made a decision to save these payments. The person saves directly by not buying the insurance, or indirectly by finding an employer not providing the coverage.

Under collateral offset, the person guarding against risk is penalized. The award from other sources is subtracted. The total amount received is the same as for the person with no insurance. The insured person is worse off, since the premium payments were made previously. Collateral offset provides incentives for persons not to carry outside insurance. The insured are penalized relative to the uninsured.

CONCLUDING REMARKS

As part of a reform program for the tort litigation system, a group of objectives is proposed. On equity grounds, the variance in awards is to be minimized across similar claims. On efficiency grounds, the transactions costs of delivery are to be minimized, with an absence of regulatory solutions. On efficiency and regulatory grounds, there should be as little restriction as possible on the freedom to contact.

High transactions costs under existing tort rules present the potential for savings in costs of doing business, at no loss to claimants. The desire is to use the court as a last rather than a first resort. While most disputes are settled, it is the threat of government action through the courts that imposes a settlement. The pattern of court rulings determines the level of settlement. There is judicial spillover, in that a high or low level of award by judge or jury establishes a precedent for future settlements and awards.

The courts are asked to mediate disputes between private parties. The reduction of a court backlog is not solved by appointing new judges. The alternative is to move cases out of the courts, reducing the necessity for appointing new judges.[27]

To reduce the variance in the award distribution, mediation or judge-only trials are alternatives. The variance is not eliminated, since judges cannot be forced to act on precedent, and circumstances in individual cases differ. Outlier high and low awards are likely to be reduced, reducing the number of appeals and costs. Society saves by removing the government conscription associated with jury duty.

Where accidents are random, or where there is a high probability of liability on both sides, such as in motor vehicle accidents, a no fault or workmen's compensation program reduces inequity across parties. Insurance firms adjust the premium rates on automobiles where there are high statistical risks. The ability to expand a no fault system outside of motor vehicle accidents is limited. The litigation faced by business varies, so comparable cases are difficult to find. Liability is often shifted to deep-pockets defendants. No fault in one area, such as workmen's compensation, shifts litigation to areas not restricted.

Contingency fees are limited in some cases. Courts are unwilling to permit contingency fees above 50 percent of an award. These restrictions act against relatively destitute plaintiffs, because they prevent the sale of claims. Contingency fees are options on claims sold to others more able to bear the risk of litigation. Any limit on contingency fees imposes on the freedom of the individual to contract. There is little justification for restriction on contingency fees, including the 50 percent practical limit on the portion paid to attorneys for plaintiffs. An expansion is to introduce contingency fees for defense attorneys.

Punitive damage awards discourage a defendant, usually a firm, from inappropriate behavior. Such damages are a fine, and more appropriately belong to a public agency, or the court itself. Punitive damages and pain and suffering limits do not impose on the right to contract. These awards are noneconomic, and not directly quantifiable, but can be imposed on corporate defendants with limited liability.

Filing fees should reflect the cost of providing and delivering service. These fees would be increased to reflect the average costs of operating the courts, including opportunity costs. *Per diem* charges would apply in cases going to trial, potentially being levied against one of the parties.

As a compensation mechanism, an English Rule with no limit on contingency fees is an alternative. This rule applies only if a case goes to court. The defendant makes a settlement proposal, to be filed with the court at least 48 hours before the start of a trial date. The plaintiff does not have to make a settlement proposal. If there is no settlement, the subsequent award is used to determine the prevailing party. If the award exceeds the offer by the defendant, the plaintiff prevails. If the award is below the offer of the defendant, the defendant prevails. The prevailing party is awarded legal costs.

The recovery of legal fees, for both the plaintiff and defendant, is based on a preset schedule of contingency fees, based on the differential between the actual award and the settlement proposal. No time spent is compensable, saving the administration and monitoring costs of the court. The courts can impose a contingency fee schedule as a procedural rule for those who have availed themselves of its services.

The defense attorney is discouraged from meter ticking activity, or delay to increase the hourly billing time. The attorney for the plaintiff has an incentive to settle. The court contingency fee upon a loss is likely to be lower than a freely negotiated fee. Because there is a risk of losing the case, and paying legal defense fees, a deduction from the award is made.

This analysis is of the legal system in the United States. Business defends against litigation in product, financial, and input markets. Of more concern are the incentives for a firm to litigate rather than produce. A firm facing foreign competition finds it more productive to engage in battle in the courts, rather than produce goods more cheaply.

The costs of litigation have been increasing. Since the consequence of awards is to reward a small number of plaintiffs substantially, overall income distribution in the United States becomes more unequal. The social climate, as the theme throughout this study, sets the level of costs. More litigation implies that the United States is likely to become less innovative in risky areas.

The costs of tort litigation include monopoly profits because some industries, notably in vaccines, are reduced to a single supplier. Distortions arise in prices that include large transactions costs.

Public policy in tort reform has been inconsistent. The focus on large awards has spawned attempts to control such settlements. Restrictions on contingent fees make plaintiffs with potentially large claims more willing to settle. Large awards are not necessarily inappropriate, and victims in these cases are undercompensated by restrictions. At the other end of the scale, there are few disincentives to bringing court action against defendants. The activities associated with the legal system consume resources, and these have an opportunity cost.

Tort reform has been manifested in a series of measures adopted by states, and proposed at the federal level. States have restricted non-economic damages and contingency fees, notably in medical malpractice cases. Joint and several liability has been restricted on noneconomic damages. Some deserving claims are restricted, with contingency fees.

More crucially, the variance and risk in awards have not been the focus of reform. The variance is a source of inequity between similar claimants, and increases the incentive to litigate. A high variance leads to the use of the court system, or its threat, to mediate disputes.

APPENDIX

Model of Contingency Fees

The model of contingency fees has the following notation: p, probability of positive recovery; A, award, if positive recovery; w, attorney hourly wage; L, attorney hours; H, defense attorney hours; λ, contingency fee; $p(L,H)A(L,H)$, expected recovery. In a Cournot-Nash equilibrium, there is noncooperation between plaintiff and defense. The probability of payoff p incorporates the optimal level of effort of the defense attorney. Let this optimal level of effort be H^*. Then the payoff function is $pA(L,H^*)$.

Hourly Wage Contract

Suppose the plaintiff retains the attorney on an hourly wage contract. The attorney works L hours, and is paid an hourly wage w. The net income of the plaintiff is

$$\pi(w,H^*)=\max_L p(L,H^*)A(L,H^*)-wL.$$
$$p\partial A/\partial L+A\partial p/\partial L=w.$$

The marginal expected net recovery per hour is equal to the wage paid to the attorney.

The plaintiff retains the attorney, who is paid on an hourly wage. The number of hours worked on the case by the attorney for the plaintiff is determined where the expected net payoff, the product of the probability of recovery and the award, is equal to the hourly wage.

Contingency Fees

Let the contingency fees be paid at rate λ, as a proportion of the settlement. The net income of the attorney for the plaintiff is maximized by

$$\pi(w,H^*)=\max_L \alpha pA-wL$$

so $\alpha d(pA)/dL=w$. The share of the settlement is equated with the opportunity cost of time. Since $\alpha<1$, fewer hours per case are spent. The recovery of the plaintiff is lower with contingency fees.

Contingency Fee Rule II

Suppose the plaintiff maximizes the net recovery $pA(1-\alpha)$ subject to the attorney covering the opportunity cost of time. Then

$$\max_{L,\alpha,\lambda} pA(1-\alpha)+\lambda(\alpha pA-wL)$$
$$L:\ (1-\alpha)d(pA)/dL+\lambda(\alpha d(pA)/dL-w)=0$$
$$\alpha:\ -pA+pA=0$$
$$\lambda:\ \alpha pA-wL=0$$

Since $\lambda=1$, $d(pA)/dL=w$. The result is the same as for an hourly wage contract. If contingency fees were limited, another constraint in the maximization problem could be added, such as $\lambda<\lambda^*$. The addition of such a constraint would further reduce L, implying a reduction in litigation.

There are capital market constraints that prevent individuals from funding litigation directly. The cost of litigation is excluded, so the optimal level of litigation cannot be determined. The distribution of awards must be considered. The award A is random. If $f(A)$, its density function, has more weight in the tails, more litigation may be attracted. The distribution of A is determined by the litigation structure.

Model of Litigation Costs

Notation is as follows: λ, contingency fee; α, filing fee; C, total claim; A, total award, with probability distribution $f(A)$ under no-fault, award not random; H, hours worked by attorney; W, charge rate per hour by attorney; S, settlement offer.

The plaintiff expected award is

$$A = \int_0^\infty (1-\lambda)Af(A)dA - \alpha.$$

If the contingency schedule is negatively sloped in the rate, the attorney has less incentive than if the schedule is increasing in the rate of commission. There is less incentive to strive for a large award, which is the return to hiring a lawyer.

For firm costs to the defendant, the notation is as follows: H_d, hours worked (billable) by attorney; $Y(K,L)$, production function for output; $Z(R,S)$, production function for litigation response (or mandated outside activity); P, price of sold output; M, price of mandated output (but has no market). Mandated output acts as tax; but it must also be the first priority of the firm. It produces Z up to certain level before it can produce any Y ($Y>0$ if and only if $Z>Z^*$).

There is a barrier to entry. Either Z is a tax or a 'negative output'. Pollution is a negative output of firm (or a 'bad') that imposes cost on society, but reduces cost on the firm.

Mandated outputs have a market value (as opportunity costs), but act as tax on output. All firms must face these within the market, but could avoid them elsewhere.

English Rule Algorithm

Let the plaintiff and the defendant each have a reservation price. The reservation level is the minimum acceptable to the plaintiff and maximum acceptable to the defendant in settlement negotiations. These reservation prices are $R(D)$ and $R(P)$, respectively. Each side makes a final offer $O(D)$ and $O(P)$. The algorithm is

$$O(D) \geq R(P)$$
$$O(P) \leq R(D)$$
$$PEN = \min(O(D), O(P)) - AWARD)$$
$$IF\ AWARD < O(D) \leq R(P)$$
$$THEN\ NET\ (P) = AWARD - PEN$$
$$IF\ AWARD > O(P)$$
$$THEN\ NET(P) = AWARD + PEN$$

NOTES

1. The discussion of contingency fees is in McKinnon (1964).

2. A 1987 survey of California voters by the polling firm of Tarrance, Hill, Newport, and Ryan indicated that a majority favored limitations on contingency fees. When asked whether such limitations would restrict access to the courts for those with low and middle incomes, voters agreed.

3. This position is advanced by Nathan Glazer and Jethro Lieberman. The judicial branch is argued to be usurping the function of the executive and legislative branches. A pressure group wanting a policy change need not petition a legislator or a member of the executive branch. By filing a lawsuit, a court can hear any issue directly, and may award compensation to the petitioner.

4. The American Textile Machinery Association testified before the U.S. Senate Judiciary Committee on March 21, 1985, that payments were made to settle claims as "extrication costs". Two separate settlements of $13,000 and $18,000 were made when the manufacturer had not made the defective product. Settlement in such a case is preferable to the continuance of litigation.

5. Jeffrey O'Connell (1979) in *The Lawsuit Lottery* describes lawsuits as a lottery and provides data on the comparable transaction costs.

6. W. K. Viscusi (1988) in "A Workmen's Compensation Proposal" proposes the extension of the workmen's compensation scheme.

7. The plan is advocated by O'Connell (1979). In criticizing the lawsuit lottery, an unbundling of the protection services in products is proposed.

8. A. M. Spence (1974) in *Market Signalling* has argued that the separation of products requires a cost differential. Consumers must become informed about positive and nontrivial costs of making a product of good quality, as opposed to advertising. More important is the inability to deny access to litigation services, even if consumers have accepted some liability. Contributory negligence standards would permit the sale of no-insurance or low-insurance goods and services.

9. Danzon and Lillard (1984).

10. U.S. Department of Justice, Report of the Tort Policy Working Group, February 1986.

11. Schwartz and Mitchell (1970) and Danzon (1983). An alternative proposal is for an optimal fee with a two-part staff, one with fixed costs and a percentage of an overage, as proposed by Clermont and Currivan (1978).

12. The U.S. Department of Justice's Tort Policy Working Group released two reports in February 1986 and March 1987. The first, from where this conclusion arises on page 71, is *The Causes, Extent and Policy Implications of the Current Crisis in Insurance Availability and Affordability*. The second is *An Update on the Liability Crisis*.

13. The decision was rendered by the California Supreme Court in *Fein v. Peninsula Medical Group* in 38 CAL 3d 695 P. 2d 665 (1985). Data on punitive damage awards are from Peterson (1987). One hypothesis is that the payment of punitive damages to the state as opposed to the individual severely restricts such awards.

14. Usually the proceeds from a court award are not subject to taxation, so the plaintiff, in future wage loss, is receiving the present value of the before-tax as opposed to the after-tax wage income. The presence of investment vehicles where returns can be made free of taxation provides the opportunity to obtain returns higher than otherwise.

15. This argument is based on comparing the English and American rules.

16. This default option is applied in some states. In federal cases it is prohibited since the 1975 Supreme Court decision in *Alyeska Pipeline Service Co. v. Wilderness Society*, 421 United States 240.

17. Some restrictions on fee recovery have been imposed at the federal level by the U.S. Supreme Court in *Serrano v. Priest*, 509 P.2sd 1303 (1977).

18. Fee-shifting rules in federal cases for legal costs are governed by Section 68 of the Federal Rules of Civil Procedure, the offer of judgment.

19. An argument in this direction has been advocated by Harvey Rosenfield, a representative of the Santa Monica organization Access to Justice. The modified English Rule has been applied on a pilot basis in two southern California counties, excluding personal injury and wrongful death cases.

20. The polling data are from the survey of California voters in October 1986.

21. Judge H. Walter Croskey, *Los Angeles Lawyer*, September 1985, pp. 16–20.

22. Small recoveries are those in excess of the amounts handled by small claims courts, with a limit of $1,500–$2,000. In the small claims courts, parties can present their cases without attorneys present. The tort litigation system described here covers claims above small claims court jurisdiction.

23. V. Fuchs (1986) *The Health Economy*, Cambridge, MA: Harvard University Press, presents the argument for medical doctors.

24. Lipson (1984).

25. Outcomes, in gains or losses, are multiplied by decision weights rather than objective probabilities. Decision weights are lower than probabilities, except for outcomes whose probabilities are low. Gambling is likely, by both plaintiffs seeking high rewards and defendants not accepting a loss-making settlement.

26. U.S. Department of Justice, February 1986, p. 71 (see Note 12).

27. The U.S. Department of Justice, in *Justice Expenditure and Employment, 1985*, has produced estimates of employment and cost in the justice system. Costs include both criminal and civil justice administration, and the categories are not

separately distinguished. For 1979–85 total federal, state, and local justice expenditure was $45.6 billion, or 2.9 percent of all government spending. While all federal spending increased 92 percent over the period, justice spending increased 68 percent. Justice spending increased 76 percent for state and local governments, while their total spending increased 72 percent.

Federal court expenditure increased 28 percent over the period, with 237 new judges appointed to clear up court backlogs. Prosecution spending increased 295 percent, and states increased their court spending by 263 percent. Public attention is focused on the U.S. Supreme Court, whose nine-member total has been unchanged. At lower levels, there has been an explosion in the number of courts and judges.

5 Litigation and Business: An International Comparison

> You have a group of [police] officers who feel that they have been
> wronged. So they file a suit against the city and the police department.
> The only cost to them is 33¹/₃% of the award if they win. Meanwhile,
> we and the taxpayers have to defend against the suit.
>
> Chief of Police, City of Cambridge, Massachusetts,
> quoted in the *Boston Globe*, March 12, 1988

The legal system is based on social and cultural institutions. These institutions differ across jurisdictions, creating differences in the cost of doing business. There are differences between the legal systems in the United States and its main competitors, notably regarding access to courts and availability of attorneys. If producers in other countries exporting to the United States have lower legal costs, there are differences in competitiveness.

Akio Morita, the chairman of Sony Corporation, notes that the legal system is one noticeable difference between business in Japan and the United States.[1] The rate of litigation in the United States exceeds that in its competitors. In 1985 of each 1,000 disputes in the United States, 44 went to trial. The comparable rates of trial dispute resolution in Japan

Thomas Campbell and Thomas Skornia provided advice and helpful discussions for this chapter. I am grateful to Kazuo Koike of Kyoto University for discussion of Japanese labor markets. Takao Tanase of Kyoto University and Shoji Terao of the Tokyo High Court provided material on Japanese litigation, and Carl Mosk gave background on Japanese institutions.

and West Germany are 12 and 23.[2] Litigation has led to the bankruptcy
of such firms as A. H. Robins and Johns Manville. These firms may
have been appropriately forced out of operation by making unsafe
products (respectively, the Dalkon shield female contraceptive and asbestos). There is a loss of the product to consumers, and employment
skills in these industries.

LITIGATION AND COMPETITIVENESS

A survey of senior executives suggests that litigation has reduced
innovation.[3] Of these executives, principally in manufacturing, 57 percent agreed that products were not going forward because of liability
suits, and for 20 percent their own company did not proceed with a
new product.

The consequence of litigation is increased involvement of lawyers
inside the company, both as corporate and outside counsel. Firms have
increased legal audits in product development, manufacturing, and
marketing as defenses against lawsuits. Marketing presents the greatest
involvement of lawyers inside the firm, with 65 percent indicating their
use. If the liability environment is unchanged, 75 percent indicate that
lawyers would have a greater role inside their firms.

Increased regulation is not viewed as the solution. Executives do not
view regulation as a substitute for litigation. The argument that increased regulation makes products safer, reducing litigation, is rejected. They oppose greater public involvement in testing and product
evaluation. They report increases in R&D spending and product safety
as consequences of litigation.

Executives exhibited familiarity with the legal system. They criticize
jury trials. Jurors are unable to make decisions on complex product and
corporate matters. Juries resort to deep-pockets awards, and usually
these are against a corporate defendant.

There is overwhelming support for tying liability to the percentage
of fault, with 96 percent in favor of removing joint and several liability.
They favor a reform package including eliminating punitive damages
except in cases of gross negligence, imposing structured settlements as
opposed to lump-sum payments, limiting contingency fees, proposing
compulsory arbitration, and an expansion of no fault or workmen's
compensation to other areas of liability.

Liability concerns are listed as the most important reason for remaining with an existing product as opposed to introducing a new one.
This is followed by the quick-fix mentality with a focus on short-term

results, the volatile business environment with mergers and restructuring, and concerns about worker training and motivation.

Product liability and employee issues account for more than two-thirds of actual suits. Employee issues include age and sex discrimination, affirmative action, and sexual harassment. The remainder of the caseload is divided between contract disputes, liability other than product, unfair business practices, and shareholder disputes.

A comparison of litigation and innovation requires examination of the legal systems in economies competitive with the United States. These differences arise because other societies have increased the cost and penalty for access to the courts.

COMPARATIVE SIZE OF LEGAL SYSTEMS

Data on the relative size of legal professions are listed in Table 5.1. In 1986 Japan had 13,200 lawyers, or 11 per 100,000 people. The United States had 655,000 lawyers, or 279 per 100,000 people. There are more lawyers than doctors in the United States. The number of doctors in the United States in 1986 was 577,000. Following the United States in the relative number of lawyers is Britain, with less than half as many, at 114 per 100,000 people. The differential between the United States and other countries in the number of lawyers per capita exceeds that for

Table 5.1
Relative Sizes of Legal Professions, Selected Countries

	Lawyers		Judges		Prosectors	
	Total	Rate	Total	Rate	Total	Rate
Japan	39.2	28	2.8	2	2.1	2
U.S.	655.0	279	27.8	12	23.2	10
U.K.	64.1	114	28.2	50	N.A.	N.A.
West Germany	47.3	77	17	28	3.7	6
France	15.8	29	4.4	8	1.5	3

Total: Number of lawyers in thousands.
Rate: Number of lawyers per 100,000 people

Source: Ministry of Justice, Japan. Data as of April 1986.

doctors. The ratio of doctors to population in Britain is similar to that in the United States. Subtracting the number of judges and prosecutors from the number of lawyers yields private practice lawyers. Prosecutors are engaged in criminal proceedings. These are subtracted, since the concern is with civil litigation. The number of private practice lawyers is listed in Table 5.2.

There is a low ratio of lawyers to population in France. This is because under the Code Napoleon, governing civil law, the judge at trial is permitted to take a more active role. In France cases are brought before a judge, often with no lawyers present. The judge leads the evidence, cross-examines, and seeks information.[4] In Britain, the legal profession is divided between barristers and solicitors. The latter perform services such as real estate transactions and wills, and do not make court appearances or initiate litigation. Judges account for a large percentage of the legal profession. The number of lawyers available for civil court litigation is limited.

All the countries in the survey are democracies, members of the Group of Seven (G7) industrialized nations, together with Canada and Italy. The United States has more than ten times the relative number of lawyers as Japan, and at least four times the ratio of any other country. The country ranking second, Britain, includes criminal prosecutors as private practicing lawyers. With their exclusion, the comparison is more unfavorable.

Table 5.2
Private Practice Lawyers, Selected Countries

	Total	Rate	Relative Size
Japan	34,300	25	10.28
U.S.	604,000	257	1
U.K. (including prosecutors)	35,900	64	4.02
West Germany	26,650	43	5.98
France	10,000	18	14.28

Source: Ministry of Justice, Japan.

THE LEGAL SYSTEM IN JAPAN

The legal system and lawyers are the symbol of business differences between the United States and Japan. When Akio Morita observed that he could not find anything made in the United States not made in Japan, he was told to take some lawyers with him.[5] With Japan as a primary competitor, it is appropriate to examine the Japanese legal system.

Level of Litigation

Japan is a less litigious society than the United States. The number of civil cases in Japan in 1986 was 340,000, or 30 per 10,000 people. There were about 100,000 large cases where the claim exceeded $6,000. In the United States $6,000 would usually be insufficient for a claimant to attract an attorney. The claimant is better served by initiating a small claims action for a smaller amount. There are about 400,000 traffic accidents annually in Japan, but only 5,000 generate court cases. The number of tort cases is 15,000 or 0.5 cases per 10,000 people.

After World War II Japanese institutions were overhauled, and a statutory legal system put in place. During the military occupation under General MacArthur, legal and labor institutions were revamped. There are several characteristics that reduce costs. The key economic ingredient is limitation on supply and demand.

On the supply side, new entrants are limited by self-regulation from the legal profession. A proportion of the entrants is required for the criminal justice system, as prosecutors and judges. There are two effects when the supply of a service is restricted. In the immediate short run the restriction on supply, with given demand, forces the price upward. The quantity of legal services transacted is reduced. The increase in price depends on the price sensitivity or elasticity of demand for legal services. The more price-inelastic the demand, the higher the price and the smaller the reduction in quantity of legal services transacted when supply is restricted.

On the demand side in Japan, the requirements for lawyers are reduced by no-fault compensation systems for accidents and torts, notably in motor vehicle cases. Alternative dispute resolution systems outside the courts are promoted. These methods include neighborhood legal clinics, arbitration, and administrative procedures.

Supply of Litigation:
Size of the Legal Profession

Of the 34,300 lawyers in private practice in Japan in 1986, nearly all were employed in law firms. Few were employed as permanent legal counsel on the staff of corporations. The United States is increasing its relative size of the legal profession more rapidly than Japan. The existing stock of lawyers in Japan is only one-tenth as large per capita as in the United States. In the United States 39,000 new lawyers are admitted to practice each year, equal to the size of the legal profession in Japan. On a base of 655,000 lawyers the growth rate is 6 percent annually. In Japan only 500 new lawyers are admitted to practice each year because of supply restrictions. On a base of 39,200 the rate of increase is 1.3 percent. If the differential in the rates of growth continues, by the year 2000 the United States will have 20 times the relative number of lawyers. Data subsequent to 1986 indicate no evidence that this scenario will fail. The legal profession in the United States is growing faster than the trend rate of gross national product of 3 percent. In Japan the legal profession is growing at well below the trend growth rate of output of 7 percent.

In California alone 4,833 people took the bar exam in February 1988; 2,242 passed, a 46.4 percent pass rate. The bar exam is offered twice annually, in February and July. The July exam has a larger number of takers. California in 1988 had 114,200 lawyers. By adding about 4,000 lawyers annually, California is producing eight times the number as Japan, which has four times the population.

The damper on supply in Japan is imposed by difficulty in passing the bar examination. The pass rate on the bar examination ranges between 2 and 3 percent of the number of candidates taking it. Of the 500 passing the bar exam, 140 become judges and 70 prosecutors, with the remainder going into private practice. The number entering private practice is more restricted than the number entering the profession. On a base of 34,300, an increase of 290 represents a 0.8 percent annual growth rate in the number of private practice lawyers. From Table 5.1, 92 percent of lawyers in the United States are in private practice, with the remaining 8 percent serving as prosecutors and judges. If this ratio is applied to the flow of new entrants, the number entering private practice grows at 35,880/604,000, or 5.9 percent annually, compared with 0.8 percent for Japan.

Because those who fail tend to repeat the test, the average age at passage of the bar exam in Japan is 28, even though law, as in Britain, is an undergraduate degree. The length of training time increases the investment cost of becoming a lawyer. The relatively late age of entry reduces the time to recoup investments in human capital, and the rate of return to becoming a lawyer. On average it takes five years of study after the undergraduate degree to pass the bar exam.

The time spent studying has a high opportunity cost. Hiring into the *nenko* sector with lifetime employment takes place when people are in their early 20s, the same years spent studying for the bar. By studying for the bar exam, individuals lose their opportunity to become employed in large *nenko* sector firms. Firms in this rigid labor market are usually unwilling to hire those over 25. A commitment to passing the bar exam in Japan means a forfeiture of favorable alternative employment opportunities. Those who fail the exam can find employment as assistants in a corporate legal department, but they are restricted from practicing. Passage of the bar exam does not qualify a person to practice law. After passing the bar exam new graduates serve an additional apprenticeship at the National Legal Training Center. This training time increases the cost of becoming a lawyer, by raising the foregone earnings associated with practice.

The limit on supply is enforced because of mutually reinforcing reasons. Existing lawyers are opposed to an increase. The demand from the judiciary and for prosecutors remains, and restricts the number of lawyers going into private practice.

Once in the profession, Japanese lawyers do not earn as much as their U.S. counterparts, or their cohort entering the lifetime employment, *nenko* sector. In the lifetime employment sector, wages increase with experience. Lawyers earn more initially, but do not receive increases with experience. Entry is restricted, and the earnings from the legal profession are relatively low. There are no contingency fees, and few lawyers are maintained on corporate retainer by defendants.

Japan has a combination of restricted entry, high prices of filing, and full cost charges for access to litigation. Court facilities are charged at prices that reflect limited subsidies. The price of using the courts, directly or as a threat, to resolve disputes is increased relative to alternatives. The use of litigation is discouraged.

Demand for Litigation

Dispute Resolution Outside Courts

Small disputes between individuals are referred to neighborhood law clinics. These storefront clinics are staffed by trained personnel equivalent to paralegals. A representative employee is a worker who has mandatory retirement at age 55 in the lifetime employment sector. Employees accept conditions less favorable than in their previous work. The other source of recruits is among unsuccessful candidates for the bar exam. These paralegal workers complete a training program in arbitration procedures administered by the government. The staffers of the neighborhood clinics are paid by the government. The price of neighborhood legal clinics is zero, causing a shift of dispute resolution from courts. Usually no lawyers are required by the disputants.

The first channel for referral of disputes between individuals and corporations, or between corporations is outside the courts. The common strand in Japanese dispute resolution is the bypass of the court system, by using arbitration or administrative procedures. Employee disputes, such as wrongful dismissal or grievances, are administered by the Ministry of Labor pursuant to the Labor Standards Act of 1947. The terms for settling disputes are stated and enforced by the bureaucracy, acting as a mediator.

Disputes between corporations on exports or trade issues are resolved by the Ministry of International Trade and Industry (MITI). Corporations have the alternative of using arbitration to settle disputes.

Arbitrators in disputes between corporations have their fees divided between the disputants, as in the United States. The long delays in the court system, and the risk of outcomes, lead firms to put cases to arbitration. The Japanese taxpayer pays the cost of the arbitrators in the neighborhood storefronts. Lawyers have almost no role in disputes outside the courtroom, and the courtroom itself is rarely used.

Alternative dispute resolution arises from cultural pressure not to sue, not to lose face, and retain a lawyer. An executive is held personally responsible for acts of failure by the corporation, and readily admits blame. Upon the crash of a Japan Air Lines airliner, the chairman of the company resigned. When it was discovered that Toshiba had sold sensitive submarine detection equipment to the Soviet Union, the chairman resigned. This admission of responsibility is viewed as sufficient punishment. The executive is unable to obtain a comparable job elsewhere, and the corporation is punished by negative publicity in the media. Negative publicity is considered harmful enough without punitive damages. Given the risk of public humiliation, Japanese executives make every effort to minimize large-scale liability problems.

While social and cultural factors are at work, economic reasons account for the relative lack of lawyers in Japan. The institutional legal system is expensive to use. Alternative means and mechanisms are available. With high costs of access in time delays, limited availability of lawyers, and high filing fees, individuals and corporations substitute more convenient alternatives.

The hidden cost of the legal system within the corporation is largely absent. Executives do not have their agenda determined externally, by the need to respond immediately to litigation requests. Depositions and subpoenas rarely arise. Lawsuits, where they occur, do not usually name executives or officers as defendants.

Dealing with bureaucratic procedures is not eliminated, since arbitration and administrative procedures are retained. There is a direct saving in the cost of litigation and doing business. The general and administrative (G&A) budget in the Japanese firm does not include as large a legal department. Indirect costs are saved, as the hidden cost to the firm is reduced.

The Court System

Japanese civil justice bypasses the courts because of lower-cost alternatives, the high cost of access to trials, and cultural opposition. Included in these court bypasses is a limitation on jury trials, and an extensive usage of no fault compensation.

Judges hear cases in Japan; there are no jury trials. There were criminal jury trials prior to 1937, but at the option of the accused. More relevantly, there have never been civil jury trials, including tort litigation. The absence of trial by jury reduces the variation in awards that creates the incentive to litigate. Judges follow precedent in decisions, under the *stare decisis* principle. Damage compensation insurance and motor vehicle accident centers prevent litigation on traffic accidents. A major contributor to legal costs, both direct and indirect, is jury trials in civil cases. The distribution of awards has a long right tail, or a nonnegligible probability of a large judgment. A jury has little perspective on legal precedent, and can be swayed by emotional circumstances. There is a lottery incentive to litigate. In the United

States, with a judge alone presiding, randomness in outcomes is not eliminated. In Japan, with judges following precedent, the scope for increasing an award by continuing litigation is reduced. The prospect of a large or small award discourages both plaintiffs and defendants from pursuing litigation. With a low variance in awards, there is an incentive to avoid the courts entirely.

The no fault aspect of workmen's compensation is used in Japan, expanded to other tort cases. Most notably, motor vehicle accidents are covered by a no fault procedure. Benefits payable are fixed by statute, with the awards adjusted for increases in the cost of living. Liability is not assessed, and awards are made on a schedule depending on the injury suffered, up to a maximum, with compensation for full medical costs. No fault and the absence of jury trials, reduce the incentive to litigate. A Japanese disputant cannot usually obtain a better settlement by litigating. The backlog in the Japanese court system reduces litigation. Court cases take several years to come to trial. Society refuses to accommodate an explosion in litigation. There are high time costs of pursuing a lawsuit, causing a reduction in demand for the services. Casual litigation or strike suits, where plaintiffs initiate low-probability, high-payoff claims, are virtually eliminated.

For cases where Japanese litigants pursue their claims in court, there is an additional risk of unfavorable publicity. Japanese firms shun unfavorable publicity. By comparison, firms in the United States are more combative. They are willing to fight for their rights and their day in court. In the suits filed by fishermen suffering from reduced catch and the mercury poisoning from Minamata disease, there was negative publicity for the accused firms. This loss of face and reduction in public esteem imposes an additional cost to the Japanese firm of using the court system.

In Japan the civil law is national and homogeneous across the country. There is a national Supreme Court, and courts at the local, prefecture, and city levels. There are local ordinances and building codes, but no variation in legal statute affecting compensation. There is no incentive for a claimant to shop around across jurisdictions.

In the United States corporations base locational decisions, including where to place headquarters, on legal considerations. The legal system is heterogeneous. The heterogeneity creates an opportunity to benefit by relocation. While there is a benefit to the firm relocating, there need be no benefit to society. One state loses a corporate headquarters, and another state gains it. Resources are expended in searching among jurisdictions, and by states in altering laws. With heterogeneous laws there is more complexity. The firm must become familiar with laws in all jurisdictions where products are sold. These are barriers that require use of attorneys from state bars across the country.

Contingency fees, where the attorney for a plaintiff is paid a proportion of an award or settlement, are not prohibited in Japan, but are not used. Attorneys for plaintiffs are paid for time worked. The Japanese litigant is required, particularly in corporation-versus-corporation disputes, to pay an up-front filing fee proportionate to the claim. The effects of paying legal fees on a continuing basis, and filing fees, creates price disincentives to using the court system for resolving disputes. The cost of using a lawyer and of litigation is increased. The up-front filing fee covers part of the operation of the court system. The Japanese use the English Rule for the settlement and award of suits. The English Rule provides for a judge, as part of a court decision, to make a determination of a prevailing, as opposed to a nonprevailing party. The judge can decide that neither party prevails. The nonprevailing party could be a recipient of a negligible damage award from a large claim. The prospect of large legal fees being awarded against a plaintiff restricts filings to strong cases. The high cost of litigation access, on both supply and demand, implies that virtually no frivolous lawsuits are filed in Japan. Firms virtually never sue each other in Japan.

In the United States the insurance company or defendant pays a claim inclusive of an attorney's contingent fee. The fees of a successful defendant are not recoverable. In Japan cost-shifting, or a recovery of fees by a successful defendant against a plaintiff, is possible. In the United States litigation and its procedures include pretrial discovery, where depositions are filed. There is considerable out of trial and pretrial time. In Japan settlements are encouraged by judges, who frequently order and assist in settlement negotiations. Once a trial starts it continues intermittently, given schedule conflicts, and does not proceed continuously, as in the United States.

U.S. competitors in Singapore, Malaysia, and Hong Kong, with the English common law, have legal systems similar to Japan. Observed unwillingness to lose face in litigation may be the consequence of charging a price for the legal system consistent with the imposed costs. A comparison of aspects of Japanese and U.S. civil litigation is listed in Table 5.3. Other differences arise with strict liability, joint and several liability, and officer responsibility.

Some of the costs of litigation are avoidable by transferring produc-

Table 5.3
Comparison of U.S. and Japanese Civil Justice Systems

	Japan	**United States**
Jury trials	No. Judge only	Yes
Filing fees	Proportional to claim Filing bonds	Limited filing fees

Payment of attorneys

	Japan	**United States**
Plaintiffs	No contingency fees	Contingency fees[a]
Defense	Hourly	Hourly

Noneconomic damages

	Japan	**United States**
Punitive damages	No	Yes
Pain and suffering	Yes, but limited	Yes[b]

Workmen's compensation

	Japan	**United States**
On job accidents	Yes	Yes - product liability
Motor vehicle accidents	Yes	No - court torts

Supply of lawyers

	Japan	**United States**
Pass rate, bar exam	2%	40% (CA)

Cost recovery

Successful plaintiff from defendant	**Japan**	**United States**
Court costs	Yes	Yes
Legal fees	Yes	Yes

Successful defendant from plaintiff	**Japan**	**United States**
Court costs	Yes	Yes
Legal fees	Yes	No

aContingency fees are limited where the United States is a defaendant, and by several states in medical malpractice cases.
bIn the United States, some limitations are placed by states on pain and suffering damages, in medical malpractice cases. In California the limit is $250,000, set in 1975.

tion offshore. The legal system cannot be avoided by any seller in a home market. The Japanese producer selling in the U.S. market has the same liability and regulatory environment as the producer in the United States. If the legal and regulatory structure is such that there may be preferential treatment, a nontariff barrier to entry is created.

The Lower Litigation Rate in Japan

In 1986 there were 340,000 cases in Japan dealt with by district courts, of which 80 percent were contract disputes. Many contract disputes are handled without lawyers. The rate of litigation is 30 cases per 100,000 people. Large litigation, involving claims in excess of $6,000, numbered about 100,000 cases. Of every 100 cases filed, only one is brought to trial. Tort cases other than traffic accident amount to 15,000 per year, or 1.5 cases per 10,000 persons.

Both cultural and economic reasons are advanced for the lower rate of litigation in Japan as opposed to the United States. Cultural arguments center on a Japanese dislike for litigation and fear of losing face. Many Japanese grew up in small communities, where it was important to maintain harmony with neighbors. People are class conscious. Litigation is seen as disrupting class consciousness, even today. There is an embarrassment in bringing problems into public view. For defendants there is a humiliation in unfavorable publicity, and a tendency to settle disputes.

Economists have an inclination to reject such cultural arguments, or to argue that other incentives account for the observed data. Lower litigation rates in Japanese society are of recent origin. During the early 1960s there were about 15,000 motor vehicle accident cases litigated per year. The caseload declined to about a third of this level by the late 1980s. The lower rate of litigation has come about during an increase in lifetime employment in manufacturing. Lifetime employment commenced during the early 1960s. The rate of direct litigation measured in courts has declined in Japan. By comparison, the rate of litigation in the United States has increased.

One area where litigation has been reduced is in motor vehicle accidents. There are neighborhood legal consultation centers, where disputants refer motor vehicle accidents (MVAs) free of charge. These centers are established by local governments, with assistance from the national government. The MVA centers are staffed by retired workers with limited formal legal training. A similar work force could be recruited from retired military personnel in the United States. Arbitration is binding on the participants. Less than 1 percent of the cases involve a lawyer.

There is a shift of caseload from courts to mediation centers. Courts in Japan handle about 5,000 MVA cases per year. Mediation centers attached to the courts deal with another 60,000 cases. The burden of the litigation is shifted from the judges to mediators. The reduction in demand for legal personnel reduces costs. This load arises from approximately 400,000 reported MVA cases per year, and the remainder are dealt with by insurance companies.

The system works because MVA cases are handled by a no fault type system, more elaborate than comparable structures in the United States. There is standardization in the payment of claims. The compensation schedule for various injuries is prespecified. There is comparative negligence. When an accident occurs because of negligence, the system prespecifies the percentage of liability borne by each party. A schedule determines the portion of allocation of costs. If speeding is involved in an accident, then 10 percent of the fault is added to the liability of the speeder.

Noneconomic damages for pain and suffering are paid on a schedule. For example, in 1987, if an accident victim is hospitalized, the person is paid ¥3000 per day, or about $25 per day at the prevailing exchange rate. The pain and suffering schedule for the loss of a leg is ¥1.5 million, or about $12,000.

The injured person is paid full medical expenses and lost wages up to a limit. Specified compensation is paid for pain and suffering. More relevant is not the level but the variance of compensation. This variance is virtually eliminated, so a claimant has no incentive to litigate. The book of payments for noneconomic damages is revised each year, to allow for inflation. There has been an attempt to apply the system to medical malpractice, but because of the heterogeneity of cases it is less successful than for motor vehicle accidents.

In Michigan, among victims of traffic accidents surveyed, 80 percent felt that they did better by hiring an attorney. This response is after the payment of 30 to 40 percent of the award in contingency fees. In Japan over 50 percent said that they did worse, on a net basis after the payment of legal fees. The relatively small number of judges and lawyers implies that there are court delays on actions filed. These delays provide incentives for parties to settle.

NONTARIFF BARRIERS: PRODUCTS AND
FIRM CASE STUDIES

Sony Corporation

Sony Corporation claims that its attempt to enter the U.S. market for television sets was affected by legal harassment. Sony's problems with the legal and regulatory system commenced in 1968 and lasted through 1975. Sony was known to be the seller of the most expensive television sets in the United States. Nevertheless, it was grouped with other Japanese suppliers in charges of undercutting prices of television sets. Three actions were brought against Sony and other Japanese television importers. Dumping charges were filed by the Electrical Industries Association with the Justice Department under federal anti-dumping regulations. Proceedings continued until 1975, when they were dismissed.

The Revenue Act of 1916 permits private lawsuits and treble damages in competition cases. Emerson, a domestic producer, filed a dumping lawsuit, which was ultimately dismissed. The third action was brought to the International Trade Commission, which obliged the Japanese MITI to limit and allocate exports of television sets to the United States.

The tribunals and courts in the United States can be accessed by an individual firm or association at low or negligible cost. The public pays the cost of investigation and administration through taxes. The costs of doing business in the United States are increased. The courts and tribunals act as a nontariff barrier. These regulatory costs emerge as value added in the United States. If the consequence is increased prices and reduced availability of television sets through the export limit, consumers pay higher prices than otherwise.

The cost to Sony was legal fees, and a distraction for the company. The litigation removes control of business from managers. At one point during the Emerson lawsuit, Sony attempted to settle. Emerson was willing to accept a settlement. Ultimately it lost the case, and the firm would have benefited from a settlement. It could not accept, because its lawyers were gambling on receiving a portion of the punitive damages on contingency, and had a contractual right to approve a settlement.

DRAM Computer Chips

Litigation that increases the cost of imports via a settlement or award results in compensation of the domestic producer, including treble damages, but raises the price for users. Anti-dumping charges were introduced in 1986 against Japanese suppliers of DRAM (dynamic read only memory) computer chips, particularly those of 256 kilobytes (256K). No penalties were levied, because an agreement was reached voluntarily on limiting Japanese exports of 256K DRAMs to the United States.

The high technology sector was divided on the issue. The Semiconductor Industry Association (SIA), representing the producers of chips, was in favor of restriction on DRAMs. The indication was that pressure could be brought to open up allegedly restricted Japanese markets to U.S.-produced semiconductors generally. At the time of the restrictions, there were three U.S. producers of DRAMs: Texas Instruments, Micron Technology, and International Business Machines (IBM). IBM produced the DRAMs solely for consumption within its own computer lines.

Among U.S. computer and circuit board producers, all except IBM and Texas Instruments were substantially affected by the restrictions. Hewlett Packard was forced to delay introduction of a line of personal computer products. Expansion boards for personal computers became difficult to obtain. Prices increased substantially, and firms were obliged to reduce production, since DRAMs had limited availability in the United States. Some firms shifted production offshore, of higher value added hardware. Consequently, the import restrictions need not have had a clear positive effect on employment and output, and are likely to have reduced both.

Since Japanese producers dominated this market, the chips soon became expensive and were in short supply. Costs to users of chips, including computer hardware manufacturers, increased substantially. Since chips enter the manufacture of circuit boards, these increased in price. It became attractive to locate production of circuit boards and computers offshore, where both price and availability of chips were more favorable.

Dumping Charges

Dumping allegations trigger administrative time and costs. The defendant firm has the obligation to pay costs to deny the claim of injury.

The plaintiff firm needs only to initiate the charge, and the government acts to investigate. Any award is received by the plaintiff firm, and is not shared with the public.

The producer in Oregon is not vulnerable to an anti-dumping charge from a producer in California. The costs of production are lower in Oregon. The supplier sells at lower prices in Oregon than in California. The producer outside the United States is vulnerable to dumping charges. These activities raise costs of entry to the domestic market, as the cost of litigation is included in the price of products. Some overseas firms are prevented from entering the market, while domestic firms receive a cost advantage. Courts and administrative procedures may favor domestic producers either explicitly or implicitly. Litigation can be more rewarding than productive activity. Firms receive compensation from importers, acting as plaintiffs. They shift the burden of the plaintiff's cost to the taxpayer, and impose the defendant's cost on the competitor. The firm that is agile within the legal system, while not being an efficient producer, may be rewarded.

The insistence of U.S. firms on legalistic procedures increases the cost of doing business internationally. Texas Instruments wanted to enter the production of semiconductors in Japan. It decided on a joint venture with Japanese suppliers, where there would be a sharing of the plant output. Negotiations stalled, since Texas Instruments wanted future production level allocations in writing with guarantees. The resolution of these matters caused much negotiation, sinch such legalistic behavior almost never occurs in Japan.

THE OPTIMAL RATE OF LITIGATION

Observers in the United States have claimed that the rate of litigation is too high, but such an assertion is relative. There are incentives in the U.S. legal system that encourage litigation, such as the lack of penalty on litigants. The level of litigation expresses democratic rights, though other democracies have substantially lower rates of litigation than in the United States. Modernization and democracy can imply increased litigation, as people attempt to obtain redress.

The Japanese seek harmony, and there is a lower rate of litigation. The emphasis of the legal system is on society as a whole, rather than on the individual. There is less willingness to compensate the individual. The emphasis is to punish the offending firm by unfavorable publicity and loss of face. If there is a change in attitudes toward individual compensation, the rate of litigation in Japan can increase.

Japanese executives doing business in the United States are critical of the legal system. In Japan discussion, not litigation, is the settlement vehicle. U.S. domestic producers are not vulnerable to anti-dumping suits or other pricing actions.

A lower rate of formal litigation does not imply a lower rate of disputes, although these may be resolved in a less costly manner. The Japanese have shifted dispute resolution from the courts to two other venues, notably regulatory agencies and neighborhood legal clinics. Disputes between companies are resolved by government agencies, such as MITI and the Ministry of Finance. Japanese firms have exhibited impatience with this adminstrative guidance that regulates market shares and production, and other disputes. Firms feel that the guidance structures are less relevant in competing in overseas markets. In the Toshiba case, involving the sale of submarine detection equipment, it was government agencies rather than the legal system that intervened.

There appears to be a change in attitude toward litigation in Japan. Lester Thurow has argued that there is a difference between the United States and Japan in litigation arising from airline crashes.[6] Victims of Japan Air Lines (JAL) crashes are willing to settle, while victims in the United States pursue litigation. Upon a crash of a JAL airliner with numerous fatalities, compensation was immediately offered to the families of victims. However, a large number of victims rejected the claims and filed suit. JAL paid according to the prevailing schedule, but these claims were not accepted.

CONCLUDING REMARKS

The United States has a different method of dispute resolution from that of Japan and Western Europe. If the production of goods and services in Japan and Western Europe is subject to legal rules that are more favorable, then the costs of doing business are lower.

Some aspects of the legal system are costly. Western Europe and Japan do not have contingency fee payments to attorneys for plaintiffs. Lawyers are paid direct fees. These are restrictions that reduce the level of litigation, but by those least able to pay. Other restrictions are imposed on entry to the legal profession through passage of the bar exam. Institutions have developed to reduce the variation in awards, through no-fault structures. The reduction in variance of awards increases equity, and reduces the transaction costs of litigation.

The most clear difference is in penalties for the entrepreneurial filing of lawsuits. In the United States the filing of suits has little downside risk of loss. In Europe and Japan, with filing fees, and the prospect of awards against plaintiffs, high-risk litigation is discouraged.

Two economic criteria for the evaluation of a legal system are efficiency and equity. Efficiency entails the satisfaction of least-cost production. Equity requires that the resulting distribution of income be less unequal. Jury trials and the absence of no-fault increase inequity by compensating some extensively and others minimally for the same tort.

There is potential inefficiency in a court-based system. The delivery of services is not at the lowest cost. The transactions costs, of paying attorneys for both sides, and of paying expert witnesses, come from the amount available to plaintiff and defendant. The net amount available to the plaintiff for a settlement is reduced. Society spends resources on the administration of the justice system that are not paid to either the plaintiff or defendant.

The shift of litigation in Japan does not eliminate the cost of dispute resolution. The costs of small disputes remains in the neighborhood legal clinics, though at lower costs. Japanese firms comply with administrative guidance at public agencies. These are the costs of doing business engendered by Japanese collective preference.

NOTES

1. Akio Morita (1986) *Made in Japan*, New York: Doubleday.
2. The statistics are from Thomas Campbell in testimony to the California State Assembly sitting as a Committee of the Whole, March 15, 1987.
3. Egon Zehnder International (1987) *Corporate Issues Monitor*, Vol. II/3.
4. Hill notes that lawyers are not immune from suits by clients. Such immunity is granted in France and England. France has *avocats* and *avoués* as lawyers, but also *notaires* (notaries), who serve many of the functions of attorneys.
5. Morita (1986).
6. Lester Thurow (1985) *The Zero-Sum Society*, New York: Basic Books.

6 Regulation and the Firm

Another cost of doing business arises from compliance with regulations. In product markets, firms are regulated on health, safety, and the environment. In financial markets, debt and equity are regulated by government agencies. Debt issues are subject to banking and monetary policy regulation. Equity issues involve securities laws. Financial statements are subject to tax laws and conformity with accounting standards. In input markets, firms have regulatory standards for plant, equipment, vendor purchases, and labor.

The benefits of regulation accrue to society, through a cleaner and safer workplace and environment. Regulation in potentially hazardous products, such as pharmaceuticals, reduces the risk of side effects, and keeps quack cures off the market, where consumers are unable to make fully informed choices. There are costs of regulation. Firms subject to regulation have direct costs of compliance. Investment in scrubbers to reduce sulfuric emissions from smokestacks has no payoff in increased output, but a social return in a cleaner environment. Costs arise where the regulatory delay in approval of a drug causes additional illness. Firms have indirect costs in executive time allocated to supervising regulatory compliance. If these costs are excluded from the cost-benefit calculation, there is a higher than socially optimal level of regulation.

This chapter arises from a concern that the American executive is spending time on regulatory compliance unrelated to production. Society establishes regulations both to increase efficiency and equity in markets, and to govern their operation. The cost of regulation is under-stated if executives are spending part of their time involuntarily on mandated activities. The response to a regulatory agency, as with a court, is required to be immediate, and cannot usually be delegated.

It has been argued that regulation exhibits cyclical behavior.[1] Be-cause of the new bodies established by Congress, the 1970s and 1980s have been a period of increasing regulation. Although the trend has abated subsequently, it is from a high level. While such a measure of regulation is not complete, it indicates the extent of the problem.

Increased regulation breaks the link between the money supply and the rate of inflation. An increase in the money supply with increased regulation can lead to a higher rate of inflation. More regulation im-plies higher prices, since the cost of doing business rises. It reduces competition, since many regulations are fixed costs. When there is deregulation, prices are lowered. The benefit of regulation, in equity and redistribution, occurs elsewhere, and may compensate for the higher prices and loss of output.

The scope of regulation is broad, and covers product markets, in-puts, health and safety, and environmental concerns. To focus atten-tion, the effect of regulation is narrowed. Since the firms of interest are in the high technology sector, some regulations that affect them are addressed. Producers of computers, semiconductors, and software have a different regulatory environment than biotechnology producers.

For biotechnology firms the scope of regulation is more pronounced, in both production and sales. A detailed examination of regulation in the biotechnology sector has been carried out. It provides a case study, and is instructive as to how the job of an executive is redefined by regula-tion. The genetic engineering or biotechnology industry is associated with work on deoxyribonucleic acid (DNA), recombinant DNA (rDNA), ribo-nucleic acid (RNA), recombinant RNA (rRNA), and cell fusion. Extension of these products and isolating specific genes poses the prospect of develop-ing better strains of crops and of treating diseases.

Modified genetic engineering has been practiced for centuries by agricultural scientists, who developed varieties of plants with specific characteristics such as weather resistance and size. The difference is that previous research did not entail direct risks to the community. The risks, and the demand for regulation, arise from two areas. First, the products formed from genetic engineering are microscopic, not observ-able to the individual. Once out of a controlled laboratory environ-ment, these microorganisms pose a risk that cannot be gauged by an outside individual or firm. Second, the microorganisms have the potential to reproduce and to transmit themselves. Any risk may be multiplied.

The chapter is organized as follows. Regulations in employment and in securities issue are examined, as areas where the cost of doing business is affected for all firms. Then a case study for the biotechnology industry is developed.

REGULATORY CONTEXT

Regulation in the United States affects firms in product markets, in financial transactions, and in input markets. On the product side there is environmental regulation on emissions of effluent into the air, water, and land by the Environmental Protection Agency (EPA). The EPA is the lead agency involved in monitoring releases into the environment, in regulation of biotechnology firms. The Consumer Product Safety Commission is involved in product regulation of consumer goods.

In financial matters there are regulations of the Internal Revenue Service, as well as state and local governments, regarding taxes. The presentation of financial statements and reporting is regulated by the Financial Accounting Standards Board (FASB), and for firms doing business with government agencies, potentially by the Government Accounting Standards Board (GASB). If the firm issues securities, the Securities and Exchange Commission (SEC) is involved.

On the input side, various regulatory bodies govern the relationship between employers and employees. Civil rights disputes are administered by the Department of Justice. Some firms have affirmative action programs. The Occupational Safety and Health Administration (OSHA) takes action on health and safety concerns, including plant site inspection. Regulations carry benefits to society as a whole. The cost is higher prices and lower output.

In product markets, emissions and product safety are regulated. Litigation acts as a complement to regulation, with product liability and malpractice cases. In input markets, firms are regulated on industrial safety, work rules, and pollution control. Litigation arises with wrongful dismissal and discrimination cases. Financial regulation includes accounting and auditing, reporting to and dealings with shareholders and lenders.

There is a tradeoff between regulation and litigation. Increased inspection and monitoring of safety standards is a direct government intervention. With an increased cost of providing safety, firms have an incentive to invest in it. Society pays for the monitoring, and receives the benefits. If the monitoring is reduced below an acceptable standard, another institution, the court system, is available.

THE CONVENTIONAL PRODUCTION APPROACH

In the conventional approach the objective of the firm is to minimize the cost of producing a given level of output. Prices and the technology are given. Any restriction or regulation limits the set of outputs that can be produced, or limits the combinations of inputs. The firm continues to minimize cost within this constrained set. The regulation is exogenous, and the firm produces its same range of products, albeit under constraint.

The question is how this characterization squares with the reality on the shop floor or in the corporate boardroom. Discussion with executives on what ails business in the United States centers on two issues, regulation and litigation.

Firms with international operations have access to a given technology. Factor proportions, or the combination of labor, capital, and purchases from other firms, and their prices, vary across countries. In theory, while having the same technology, plants in different locations have different combinations of inputs to produce a given output. These combinations vary with local availability and prices. A location where labor is cheap or abundant has a more labor-intensive technology.

The same machinery is used to make semiconductors or computers in each plant, because there is a prevailing technology. Unlike agriculture, where some producers may use oxen and others tractors, the technology in manufacturing, particularly high-technology firms, is relatively uniform. What differs is how the machinery is used, and constraints and restrictions in adjusting and altering labor.

In reality, in a Third World country a multinational firm is not producing semiconductors with labor only, while producing in a fully automated plant in an industrial country. The factor proportions exhibit little variation, and location depends on the institutional environment. In services, multinational firms are more restricted on relocation than in goods production.

Regulations within an economy determine location decisions. One regulatory criterion is the extent to which the domestic market is closed to imports. This closure protects domestic production. Low value added production is subsidized by tariffs and quotas, leading to a screwdriver industry. The flexibility of a firm to adjust employment is regulated. Restrictions on layoffs or adjustments in employment increase the cost of labor. The marginal product of labor, or addition to output from hiring another worker, is specific to a location and technology. These location decisions concern process manufacturing, where little innovation in production is necessary. The location with the lowest process manufacturing cost is not necessarily that with the lowest cost in innovation. Firms or plants do not differ substantially in access to technology, or in the actual machinery or production function deployed.

An Alternative Production Approach

The reality facing a firm suggests an alternative paradigm. The firm does not have a conventional production possibility set for maximization of profit or minimization of cost under constraints. Instead, the types of goods produced, and the set of possibilities itself, depend on the institutional environment. The firm not only produces semiconductors, or a generic commodity such as dynamic read only memory chips. The DRAM maker is producing regulatory compliance, litigation response, and other services mandated by the location of production.

The set of outputs is changed. While the firm is nominally producing DRAMs, it is producing a number of other services. The cost function, minimizing across locations the cost of a given level of output, is inappropriate. There is no output aggregate. Different outputs are being produced across firms and locations. The firm efficient in producing DRAMs need not be in producing regulatory compliance or legal services.

Executives from various firms in Silicon Valley, the high-technology corridor in Santa Clara, California, argue that they spend about 20 percent of their time on regulation and litigation. These matters are tied to institutional circumstances, depending on location, and are not related to the product line. When the normally volatile stock price of a high-technology firm falls sharply, it runs the risk of a lawsuit. The lawsuit, usually a class action filed by a shareholder with limited ownership, holds the officers personally responsible.[2]

Given regulation and litigation, the cost of paying workers varies across locations, for the same plant, equipment, and material costs.

The differentials arise because of labor laws and restrictions, notably in Europe. The cost is created by explicit protection, or by nontariff barriers such as technical standards.

The U.S. government argues that it adopts the same standards toward domestic and foreign producers. In biotechnology the same tests are required for all potential suppliers. The regulatory testing accords protection to domestic suppliers. Foreign producers must supply the same type of test results to the Food and Drug Adminstration (FDA). Usually this data set requires rigorous testing with clinical trials in the U.S. market.

BENEFITS AND CONSEQUENCES OF REGULATION

There are benefits of regulation. Safety and health are useful to society, but they have a free rider characteristic. The firm investing in safety is not necessarily able to charge a higher price, or to have its workers take a lower salary than otherwise.

A fast food restaurant generates garbage and litter, sometimes in areas removed from the premises. The food sold may not be nutritious or constitute a balanced diet. The local authority is justified in regulating to ease the congestion around the restaurant and in public refuse facilities.

Since the firm has no incentive to reduce the amount of litter or chlorofluorocarbons in styrofoam packaging damaging to the ozone layer, regulations are imposed. The costs of doing business are increased. The manager may be required to spend time dealing with city governments and enforcing regulations. These costs of doing business are set against the benefits of lower levels of pollution. In calculations of the regulatory effects, the direct costs of the restaurant in higher packaging costs per unit, or in reducing packaging, are included. The time of the manager, as an indirect cost, is included. The external cost imposed on society is internalized by regulation.

The cost of regulation, notably in biotechnology, can be industrial concentration. Longer patent lives are granted. Higher barriers to entry protect existing firms and those with deep pockets. The award of longer patents provides guaranteed protection of a monopoly right. The price is increased, and output reduced.

The long lead time and the high price cause a barrier to entry. There is a reduction in innovation, since only firms with long time horizons, or patient venture capitalists, are able to wait through the process.

Firms require alternative sources of funds, such as the cash flow from existing successful products, to cross-subsidize new ventures.

If there is input and production regulation after the R&D investment, the cost of domestic production increases relative to an offshore location. Extreme process regulation, including laboratory supervision and monitoring, creates incentives to locate production overseas.

EMPLOYMENT REGULATION:
THE UNITED STATES AND JAPAN

In the United States the firm is permitted to discharge the worker deemed unproductive or disloyal. Barriers to removal of workers exist in most Western European countries by explicit regulation. In Japan there is no formal regulatory structure, but custom in large firms indicates that workers have permanent employment. The U.S. firm can remove a worker, and there is relatively high employment turnover, particularly among younger workers. Nevertheless, there are relatively high lengths of job duration. Access to litigation for wrongful dismissal permits workers to seek compensation, and potentially firms have a large liability. On the other side of the bargain, there is low loyalty of workers to firms. The adjustment to lifetime employment is to place an upper bound to the obligation that the Japanese firm.

While lifetime employment is not explicit in Japan, mandatory retirement is imposed by regulation, usually at age 55. There is delayed entry into the labor market, with firms hiring people in their early to mid-20s. These two boundaries in age reduce the potential liability for lifetime employment.

In Europe there is delayed entry through apprenticeship programs in such countries as West Germany, and the effective regulatory mechanism of high youth unemployment. The Japanese firm has an upper bound to the obligation. The United States has no comparable mandated upper bound. The direction of regulation in the United States is to increase retirement ages, to counter discrimination by age in employment.

The Age Discrimination in Employment Act of 1978 prohibits U.S. firms from enforcing mandatory retirement provisions before age 70, and even this age can be challenged. The potential obligation to hire a worker is 15 years longer than in Japan. The majority of wrongful dismissal cases in the United States has been brought not on grounds of race or sex, but by workers aged over 55. In Japan workers retire at age

55, and are willing to take jobs in the secondary, less regulated labor market. There is no mandatory retirement age for executives, though large firms have imposed an informal limit at age 65.

Retiring executives are retained as consultants, acting as a buffer to provide expertise without the obligation for the full salary. The relatively limited scope of government programs tied to employment, such as unemployment compensation, implies that workers remain with firms. They are not subsidized to search for jobs, or to delay accepting a job while awaiting a better offer.

Japanese firms do not view sales jobs as demeaning. Given long-term employment, engineers and scientists are encouraged to enter sales, to obtain familiarity and belief in the product, and to build loyalty. Sales positions are more specialized, and workers are not rotated between sales and production. There are exceptions, notably in firms that offer lifetime employment akin to the Japanese system, such as at IBM. At some firms sales jobs are used as worker disciplining mechanisms. An employee is effectively offered lifetime employment, but those redundant in a production or general and administrative area are assigned to sales, where compensation on commission reduces the direct obligation of the firm.

The phenomenon of lower worker loyalty in the United States at the managerial level may be partly attributable to the method of training. Those with graduate business degrees are taught general managerial skills. These skills are transportable across industries, and the recruiting process promoted by the schools encourages students to seek employment wherever short-term rewards are highest.

In Japan wages are based on seniority and experience. There is an incentive to strive for promotion and a long-term reward. Short-term productivity is not immediately rewarded, but is recognized in the future. Workers are "underpaid" in the early years, but are "overpaid" later as rewards for earlier loyalty and hard work.

The Japan Labor Standards Act of 1947 and subsequent legislation mandate workmen's compensation and establish employment conditions. A worker injured on the job receives 60 percent of salary up to a limit, after 10 months of employment. These benefits are not taxed. There is a statutory maximum to the industrial workweek at 48 hours, with the actual average at 43 hours. Provisions of the Labor Standards Act are administered by the Ministry of Labor.

The mandated administration of the Ministry of Labor and lifetime employment among large employers ensures that there is virtually no litigation on employment matters, such as wrongful dismissal or termination. Administrative guidance from the Ministry of Labor and bureaucratic procedures are used to solve employee grievances.

New products and development ideas percolate upward via the proposal system. Middle managers are directly involved in innovation decisions. Since middle managers know that under the lifetime employment system they will eventually be senior executives themselves, they have more interest in developing products of value to the firm.

There are problems with the Japanese labor market. The high cost of a mistake in hiring into the *nenko* system, with firms forced to carry an unproductive 23-year-old until age 55, leads to a reluctance to hire. Prospective employees are obliged to invest in market signals, observable characteristics correlated with productivity, such as degrees from the most prominent universities or the right preschool. Parents invest in *juku*, additional classes for children, to ensure that they enter the appropriate educational track.

The risk of error makes firms unwilling to take a chance with workers whose variance of productivity is high. Women and minorities, such as those of Korean origin, are restricted in employment opportunities. The rapid growth rate of output and a low unemployment rate do not translate into increased employment for these groups. The adjustment is to increase the productivity of those already employed, as opposed to increasing the number of employees.

Firms restrict the freedoms of workers, and reduce their choices, to enforce the provision of lifetime employment. Japanese firms take Draconian measures that would be unacceptable in the United States. If adapted in the United States, they would not necessarily lead to more productive behavior by workers. There is uneasiness about the mobility of workers in the United States, where workers take corporate secrets and plans with them. Japanese firms introduce corporate socializing, often at a company-owned club where only other employees are permitted. These restrictions may make workers less creative, or less willing to undertake new projects.

COMPARATIVE REGULATION IN JAPAN

In Japan the bureaucracy serves a guidance and regulatory function. In the United States the bureaucracy acts as a policing agency. This function is exercised notably by agencies such as the Securities and Exchange Commission and the Federal Trade Commission. These agencies act to regulate and to enforce laws, and not to mediate disputes between firms. A natural hostility between business and government arises because of the policing function. This hostility is manifested in an unwillingness to cooperate with regulatory structures.

Japanese business relies on self-regulation. Corporate failure is deemed to be a disgrace. Usually these executives cannot be re-employed, since another firm wants to hire at the bottom in the seniority system. A high cost is associated with a public failure. There is a disciplining force acting to increase quality control and performance. A system where the failed manager cannot be employed elsewhere makes for both loyalty and a low tolerance for errors.

It is argued that in Japan firms have an objective of making workers happy, in terms of amenities and social facilities. Since workers are long-term assets, the firm has a greater incentive to invest in them. In the United States, where the objective is profit maximization, there is less emphasis on employees. Turnover of workers reduces the willingness of firms to invest.

FINANCIAL MARKET REGULATION
AND EXECUTIVE COMPENSATION

The regulatory environment determines whether a firm becomes private or is publicly held, and the issue of securities. A firm offers an Employee Stock Ownership Plan (ESOP) to an executive or other manager permitting the option to purchase stock, as part of the compensation package. The manager can take a job with a competitive firm offering a higher salary and no ESOP. Where capital gains receive preferential tax treatment, the firm has an additional incentive to shift total compensation toward stock options and other equity, as opposed to salary. Where the rate of capital gains taxation is increased, the firm reduces the price the executive pays for the option. If the stock is issued as treasury shares, or as a new issue, the remaining shareholders subsidize the stock option. If the firm purchases the stock in the open market for resale to the executive, existing shareholders benefit from the increased demand for the stock.

There are incentive reasons why firms issue stock options to reward executives. Incentive issues include making the executive feel more a part of the firm. The performance of the firm affects the reward to the manager, creating incentives to maximize the price of the stock.

There are regulatory inconsistencies. A stock option or ESOP is a substitute for a pension plan, although firms may offer both benefits. Equity offerings to employees are part of compensation in the United States, just as the bonus is part of compensation in Japan. The incentives of firm and employee are made consistent. The fortunes of the employee are tied more closely to the firm. The ESOP is a substitute for a pension plan that conveys no external cost on public funds. The firm has no unfunded pension liability, such as the pension plan of government employees.

There is no attempt to shift the cost elsewhere, as occurs with pension dumping onto the Pension Benefits Guaranty Corporation (PBGC). Under the Employee Retirement Income Security Act (ERISA) of 1974, a levy is applied to private pension plans, to guarantee the benefits of retiring and retired employees. If a firm declares bankruptcy, benefits are paid to the workers through PBGC. Firms have an incentive to award benefits they are incapable of honoring, and to shift their pension benefit obligations to the public treasury. If there is a subsidy from general tax revenues, firms not offering a direct pension plan assist in paying for employees with a pension plan.

If a firm develops an ESOP as an alternative to a pension, or as a supplement, employees stand to run afoul of securities legislation geared more at investors than employees. An ESOP has a set of incentives different from a pension. Employee stock options reward current productivity, and pay for creative talent immediately. Pension benefits pay only after retirement, rewarding loyalty.

The employee with the ESOP has a call option. This option provides the right to buy the stock of the company at a given price, at a given date. An American option can be exercised at any date prior to maturity. A European option is exercisable at maturity. The employee exercises the options at the due date. Since cash is required to exercise the option, one strategy is to sell a portion of the stock immediately, using the capital gains from the option to pay for the remaining stock held.

The employee has an option to buy 1,000 shares of the stock for $30 when the market price at the exercise date is $40. The option price at exercise date is $10. It costs $30,000 for the employee to exercise the option. By selling 750 shares immediately into the market, $30,000 is received. The employee holds the remaining 250 shares, and is not out of pocket in the transaction, barring any brokerage or other fees, or assuming they are borne by the company. The remaining 250 shares represent $10,000 in compensation.

The employee runs into several regulatory problems in the transaction. Insider trading regulations are applicable. Insiders are all employees and shareholders with access to information not available to the public. Under Section 16B of the Securities Act, insiders are required to have a six-month no trading period. If the employee cannot raise $30,000 by a method other than sale, the option may be unexercisable.

There are tax implications. The capital gain from the exercise of the option is taxed as ordinary income. The exercise of a stock option is a tax preference item, subject to the Alternative Minimum Tax (AMT). Under the AMT, deductions against income are restricted. This provision reduces the incentive to pay an employee entirely in stock options to avoid taxation. At exercise of the option, a tax is payable. In the example there is $10,000 of taxable income from the exercise of the option, and this is subject to the AMT.

Regulatory provisions and tax policy reduce the benefit of the ESOP. The firm responds by lowering the exercise price of the option, but this results in higher costs of compensation. The insider trading policy provides problems for senior executives and officers. Their holdings are immobilized. If they attempt to sell, they can be investigated for engaging in insider trading, particularly if the stock falls. A movement in either direction of the price can trigger regulatory activity.

Without regulations it would be rational for an employee to take the stock options, sell them into the open market, with the income part of compensation. Since the employee is subject to insider trading regulations, the stock is held, and the employee borrows to fund the purchase.

Securities regulations discourage other appropriate behavior by executives or employees. It is prudent to diversify a portfolio. An individual has financial assets, of stocks, cash, and other negotiable instruments, physical assets, and human capital. The human capital is the skills used to earn wages and salaries. The employee rents human capital to the firm during a pay period. Since time and restrictions make it difficult to have more than one employer, the employee has an undiversified human capital portfolio. The job risk is reduced if the employee hedges, by selling short the stock of the employer. The more senior the executive, or the greater the perceived risk, the more short selling. If options in the stock are available, the employee sells a call option, or buys a put option. A put option entitles the holder to sell the stock at a given price. If options are part of the ESOP, the employee exercises them and sells the stock short.[3] Apart from perceptions of disloyalty, this strategy is likely to violate regulations on insider trading.

REGULATION AND THE BIOTECHNOLOGY INDUSTRY

Approval of a New Drug

Regulation of drugs sold in the United States dates to 1937. The drug elixir sulfanilamide was sold, and up to that date no clinical testing on new products had been carried out. Elixir sulfanilamide had passed no tests, and there were 100 deaths in two months.

Pressure for regularity legislation led to the passage in 1938 of the Food, Drug and Cosmetics Act. New drugs had to pass tests, administered by the FDA, established by the act. Under the 1938 Act, the Investigational New Drug (IND) procedure was required. Filings were required for new drugs with the Food and Drug Administration, created by the act. The restrictions were imposed after birth defects were associated with thalidomide, which was taken in Europe during pregnancy.

Thalidomide was never licensed for sale in the United States, not having satisfied existing regulations. In response to the thalidomide cases in Europe, the 1962 Kefauver Amendments to the Food and Drug Act of 1938 were passed. The Kefauver Amendments required a New Drug Application (NDA) in addition to the IND. Under the NDA the producer must prove that the drug is "efficacious". Double-blind testing is required, with statistically significant results in various locations. In the double-blind testing some patients must be given a placebo, but not be informed.

The benefit of the regulatory lag, up to ten years for a new drug, is that unsafe products are kept off the market. The cost is higher prices for drugs on the market, and delays in treatment of sufferers. Smaller firms are restricted from entry. Exceptions arise in firms spawned from research laboratories at universities and governments, where public funds are invested in the risk-taking.

The structure of drug approvals in biotechnology is a case study. A new drug involving recombinant deoxyribonucleic acid (rDNA) and microbial isolation is regulated by the FDA. The FDA checks whether the cloned DNA is properly identified. The details of the construction of the organism must be publicly available. The inserted DNA is verified as "well characterized." "Well characterized" in regulations means that the producer can document the exact nucleotide sequence of the insert and any flanking nucleotides.

Regulation depends on pathogenic characteristics. A pathogen is a virus or microorganism that has the ability to cause disease in other living organisms. A microorganism is included if it belongs to a pathogenic species. A nonpathogenic strain of a species containing a pathogenic strain is *Escherichia coli* K-12. The screening structure is described in Table 6.1.

Preclinical studies are then performed in test tubes and lab animals. The company files an Investigational New Drug report with the FDA once these tests have been completed. Regulations on the use of lab animals at federal, state, and local levels are complied with. Once the FDA approves the IND, the company begins studies on both healthy

Table 6.1
Structure of Regulatory Approval for New Drugs in the United States

Stage	Time
1. Synthetic chemical screened for potential use	
2. Pre-clinical studies in test tubes and lab animals	2 years
3. company files Investigational New Drug (IND) with Food and Drug Administration (FDA)	
4. Clinical studies in healthy humans and patients	2 years
5. Large clinical studies	3 years
6. Company files New Drug Application (NDA) for review by FDA (studies showing effects of clinical trials). Document processing at FDA	3 years
7. Drug approved for marketing	
Total (including steps 1., 3., and 7.)	up to 10 years

humans and patients. Some healthy persons and sufferers of the disease are given the drug; others are given a placebo. The testing on humans in clinical studies takes two years.

The next stage is to replicate these studies on larger samples of healthy and ill humans, over three years. At this stage the company files a NDA at the FDA. The FDA reviews the large- and small-scale tests before the company begins studies on healthy humans and patients. Some healthy persons and sufferers of the disease are given the drug; others are given a placebo. The testing on humans in clinical studies takes two years.

The next stage is to replicate these studies on larger samples of healthy and ill humans, over three years. At this stage, the company files a NDA at the FDA. The FDA reviews the large- and small-scale clinical studies. It is at this stage that criticism of the agency has been levied. The FDA takes up to three years to review the material. Its reasons for rejection, or requiring more tests, are considered to be arbitrary. In the meantime, people continue to suffer with the disease. Once this document processing has been approved by the FDA, the drug is marketed.

AIDS and New Drugs

A change of attitude has developed with Acquired Immune Deficiency Syndrome (AIDS). In October 1987 the state of California overrode federal FDA regulations for AIDS drug testing. AIDS drugs not federally approved can be tested on patients within California. The FDA revised its classification testing to speed approval of anti-AIDS drugs. A classification 1-AA applies only to AIDS drugs, reducing the approval time. The policy argument is that unlike cancer or heart disease, the other high cost per case illnesses in the United States, AIDS can be spread by a carrier, and is fatal. By putting AIDS drugs on the market, the lives of sufferers can be extended, or made less painful, and potentially the spread of the disease reduced. Under this 1-AA classification, the drug azidothymidine (AZT) (Burroughs Wellcome of Research Triangle, North Carolina) was approved for use on patients. AZT modifies the symptoms of AIDS to increase the life span of those with the disease.

The document-processing phase, normally up to three years, was reduced to four months. While AIDS drugs receive the highest priority, other drugs have received rapid approval. Lovastatin by Merck, a cholesterol-reducing drug, was approved in nine months.

Some criticism has been directed at the IND and NDA procedures regarding AIDS. If there is no known cure for a disease, it has been argued that there is no cost to using an experimental drug on patients. The NDA procedure delays the marketing and testing of drugs. The converse argument is that any cures could then be marketed, and sufferers would have no means of distinguishing effective treatment. Quack cures are held off the market, since their promoters are less willing to make the investments in testing and research.

Regulation in Genetic Engineering

Regarding DNA, rDNA, RNA, and rRNA, public regulation has centered on the difference between intergeneric and intrageneric combinations. Intergeneric combinations are deliberately formed microorganisms containing genetic material from dissimilar source organisms. Intrageneric combinations are microorganisms formed by genetic engineering other than through intergenetic combinations. A pathogen is a virus or microorganism, including its viruses or plasmids, that has the ability to cause disease in other living organisms. Living organisms include animals, humans, and microorganisms.

The focus of regulation is on intergenetic combination. A microorganism is excluded from regulation if it is well-characterized and contains non-coding regulatory regions where an intergeneric combination can be excluded from regulation. Well-characterized means there is documentation of the exact nucleotide base sequence of the regulatory region and any inserted flanking nucleotides; that the regulatory region solely controls the activity of other sequences that code for protein or peptide molecules; and that the regulatory regions and any inserted flanking nucleotides do not code independently for a protein, peptide, or functional RNA molecule.

The exclusions are those with no coding capacity for production, reproduction, or proliferation of a gene product. The danger to the environment is minimized. Those products excluded under the well-characterized condition are promoters, operators, terminators, origins of replications, and ribosome binding sites. These elements are responsible for the nucleic acid synthesis at the specific region where they appear in the chromosome.

Bacterial genes are based on a series of regulatory elements. The principal unit is the operon. The operon is controlled primarily by regulation of the rate of initiation of messenger RNA synthesis. This

regulation is based on the interaction between the operator and promoter, two nucleotide sequences in the DNA. The promoter is the site
of RNA polymerase binding. The operator is the on–off switch for the
movement of polymerase into the structural gene that follows immediately behind. The operator binds a cellular processor protein synthe-
sized in response to nutritional stimuli. Terminator regions are short
nucleotide sequences that signal the dissociation of the polymerase
from the DNA.

In all current cases the replication of DNA is initiated at a specific
site or group of sites in a chromosome. These are specific sites, and a
DNA molecule without the appropriate site is not replicable. The origin of DNA replication is a short nucleotide sequence, the initiation site
for a specific enzyme action. For mammalian DNA to replicate in
bacteria, it must be associated with a bacterial origin of replication
and vice versa.

Ribosome binding sites are short nucleotide segments at the begin-
ning of messenger RNA molecules that signal the attachment of ribo-
somes for the initiation of protein synthesis. Functioning in this role,
they are not translated into the protein or peptide being processed.

Issues in Biotechnology Regulation

Regulation Not Providing Immunity

Regulation guards the public health and safety against risks. In genetic engineering, public risks are associated with the reproduction of
microorganisms. The long regulatory cycle and procedures are imposed
to reduce these risks. The approval of a product by any regulatory
agency does not bring immunity from additional costs of litigation.
Regulation imposes a cost on the firm. It brings patent protection, but
no protection against litigation. The firm is unable to use as a sufficient
defense its satisfaction of and compliance with government regulations. There is compensation to the firm in increased patent protection,
but this conveys a monopoly profit, and there are losses in output and
higher prices. Under the 1965 Second Restatement of Torts, "compliance with legislative enactment or an administrative regulation does
not prevent a finding of negligence." There is no substitution of regulation for litigation. Rather, the firm has higher costs for compliance,
and a continuing risk of litigation.

Regulatory Asymmetry

There is an asymmetry in regulation. Genetic alteration causes the regulatory process to be triggered. Similar products that arise from chemical alteration, or through exemptions in regulations, as for well-characterized products, have less restrictive regulation.

Regulation imposes an artificial tradeoff. The biotechnology firm invests in genetically altered microorganisms, knowing that there is more regulation, a longer lead time, and higher start-up costs. The benefits are protection against competitors who have similar regulatory costs and lack identical patents. The increased monopoly profits from the publicly awarded patent are balanced against a higher regulatory cost. The alternative is to invest in chemically altered products that have lower start-up costs and shorter research and development periods. The costs are lower, but the benefits of monopoly profits are restricted.

The tightest regulation is on recombinant DNA (rDNA) and RNA (rRNA). Some of these products are biologically similar to those developed chemically. The only difference is the technology of production. A firm can produce a given product either by using rDNA, or by a chemical process. If rDNA is used, it is regulated, but if the chemical process is used, there is less regulation. Input or production regulation leads to higher costs of producing similar outputs.

Regulatory Overlap

Regulatory overlap affects biotechnology. Approval by the U.S. Department of Agriculture Safety and Environment (USDASE) group is required if there is agricultural use, or if the product contains a serum or toxin. Toxic substance control is administered by the Environmental Protection Agency (EPA), and the Occupational Health and Safety Administration (OSHA) if workers are exposed. There is state and local control on test sites and at laboratory locations. Even if federal agencies have given permission, experimentation and location of test sites may be restricted.

One area of contention is a definition of "release into the environment" of a microorganism. Since these microorganisms have the potential of reproduction, and the consequences are unknown, external release has been regulated. The definition of a release varies across agencies.

The issue of regulatory overlap in genetic engineering has had productive results. A coordinated framework for the regulation of biotechnology has emerged. The restructuring of regulatory authority, as formulated by the Office of Science and Technology Policy, and published in the *Federal Register* in 1986, is to reduce but not eliminate the overlap. The structure of regulation is described in Table 6.2.

An attempt has been made to develop a lead agency in each area whose regulations dominate. The NIH continues to formulate regula-

Table 6.2
Coordinated Framework, Biotechnology Research Jurisdiction

Contained Research, No Release to Environment (not Federally Funded)	NIH, USDASE
Foods, Food Additives, Human Drugs, Drugs, Medical Devices, Biologics, Animal Drugs	FDA, EPA
Plants, Animals and Animal Biologics	APHIS, USDASE

Pesticide Microorganisms

Genetically Engineered

Intergeneric	EPA, APHIS, USDASE
Pathogenic Intrageneric	EPA, APHIS, USDASE
Nonpathogen Intrageneric	EPA, USDASE

Nonengineered

Nonindigenous Pathogens	EPA, APHIS
Indigenous Pathogens	EPA, APHIS

Microorganisms Released into the Environment

Genetically Engineered

Intergeneric, Commercially Funded	EPA, APHIS, USDASE
Intragenetic, Commercially Funded Pathogenic (Source Organisms)	EPA, APHIS
Nonpathogenic	EPA

Nonengineered	EPA

Notes: NIH, National Institutes of Health; USDASE, United States Department of Agriculture, Safety and Environment; FDA, Food and Drug Administration; EPA, Environmental Protection Agency; APHIS, Animal and Plant Health Inspection Service.

tions on food and health products, but the EPA and the two agricultural agencies assume primary responsibility.

The regulatory delays imposed on new products cause high fixed costs of production. The cost of compliance arises early in the product cycle, where there is no revenue. This restricts the entry of start-ups into the drug and pharmaceutical industry.

Case Studies

Genentech

This section reports on two firms involved in genetic engineering and their interaction with regulations. Genentech, of South San Francisco, California, markets tissue plasminogen activator (TPA), a genetically engineered product. It is also sold under the trade name Activase. TPA dissolves blood clots that follow heart attacks. While tests had been performed, the company did not know the market demand or effectiveness of the drug. These are appropriate business risks, evaluated in obtaining venture capital and equity funding.

After the IND process and eight years of investment, research, and development, but no revenue for Genentech, the FDA turned down approval of TPA in May 1987. The FDA argued that more studies were required. In a sudden reversal of decision, and with no more studies or data supplied, in October 1987 the FDA permitted TPA to be marketed.

There is randomness in the approval decision, and a policy risk associated with regulation. Because of the regulatory cost, provision for litigation, and the monopoly power conveyed, Genentech commenced the charge for TPA in May 1988 at $2,200 for an annual dosage.

For drug products restrictions by third-party providers prevent the payment of high prices. The diagnosis-related group (DRG) program under the federally funded Medicare and Medicaid programs establishes maximum payments for specific illnesses and treatments. Since arguable substitutes were available at $500 per year, or with no drug intervention, federal programs imposed restrictions on purchase of TPA.

Another problem lies in regulatory overlap. Another Genentech product, bovine interferon, was delayed because of conflict over agency jurisdiction. Since it was derived from cattle, the U.S. Department of Agriculture Safety and Environment (USDASE) claimed a regulatory responsibility. The USDASE licensed the drug as a "veterinary biologic", but the FDA classified it as a "new animal drug", with each classification requiring different standards. After attempting to negotiate with the two agencies, the product was licensed to a Swiss firm, Ciba-Geigy, in 1985, where testing has continued under the aegis of the FDA.

Advanced Genetic Sciences

Another genetic engineering firm, Advanced Genetic Sciences, developed a frost-suppressant bacterium. Genes were deleted from a common plant bacterium. Then a test was performed to see how the organism had been altered. Some strawberry plants were sprayed with the bacterium to determine the reduction in risk of frost damage. The frost suppressant was also injected into the bark of fruit trees in Oakland, California.

The spraying was required to conform to a definition of a release into the environment. The sprayed fields were on a test plot, since laboratory tests had already been performed. The release complied with NIH, but not with EPA guidelines. Because of failure to comply with the EPA guidelines, the company was fined and required to repeat the experiment inside a greenhouse, where potential release could be controlled.

The publicity from the case raised the concerns of local governments. The city of Monterey refused permission for the test. Even when the EPA gave permission, and a test site was selected, environmental authorities of the state of California imposed restrictions on the spraying. The workers were required to wear sealed moonsuits, helmets, and gloves.

The effective concentration of regulation in the hands of the EPA need not solve all problems associated with biotechnology. It may result in the shift of focus to litigation. Under the 1969 National Environmental Policy Act (NEPA) courts are empowered to review the actions of any government agency that have significant effects on the environment. Even if an agency of the government has approved an experiment, individuals can file suit under NEPA to block testing.

The Advanced Genetic Sciences case was affected by NEPA. Once the regulations on spraying had been advanced, a suit was filed under NEPA. The firm was giving consideration to carrying out the testing and spraying offshore.

In California a public initiative provides for those bringing an environmental action to be paid a 25 percent bounty. This bounty hunting promises to increase the quantity of litigation in this area. The act requires that an environmental impact report on flora, fauna, and all human environments be conducted, and that extensive reviews be performed.

CONCLUDING REMARKS

Regulation aims to promote the public health and safety, by increasing compliance costs of firms. If regulation focuses on the input or production side, and becomes excessive, firms choose to reduce or remove production. Employee work rules that are strict in one location are balanced by a reduction in production.

In the pharmaceutical and drug industry, there are inconsistencies with regulation. If regulation creates a monopoly there is a deadweight loss absorbed by the community. In biotechnology, local government approval is involved in test permission. The case of Monsanto is instructive. The black cutworm is a pest to corn. Monsanto developed a black cutworm suppressant. To control the black cutworm, the company inserted a gene into a microbe, so a protein lethal to the parasite could be created. The testing was opposed by St. Charles, Missouri, even though it was not in the county of activity. In Illinois the company was permitted to carry out the same tests, inserting the same gene into tomato plants.

NOTES

1. R. N. Batra (1986) *The Great Depression of 1990*, New York: Simon & Schuster.

2. Class action lawsuits are discussed in Chapter 3.

3. Such an employee may be viewed as disloyal. It may be appropriate in sectors of the economy where there is high turnover and risk of job loss.

7 Market Forces and the Firm

This chapter examines the market as an institution imposing external costs. Market forces may distract managerial attention without improving productivity. The types of externally imposed dislocations are associated with employee benefits and financial markets. For employee benefits such as health care, the price charged the user is below the total cost of the service. The employee does not include total costs in decisions on usage. This generated demand increases the cost of health benefits, and of doing business. Firms paying the cost are forced to cross-subsidize between workers. Some workers receive large benefits, because of their health status and number of dependents. These benefits are unrelated to the value of the employee to the firm.

Other aspects of market behavior have negative impacts on firms. One area examined is trading in securities. Some strategies shift the risk from one group of shareholders to another. If the group that is receiving the risk includes employees, there is an increase in the cost of doing business.

Externally imposed costs for the firm arise through the market directly, or because of a failure of provision for public services. For business in the United States, a large cost item is health care. For large employers, the average per employee health cost in 1987 was $1,985.[1]

The focus in previous chapters has been on the CEO, and the reaction of the firm to externally imposed costs. A regulatory hearing, at the legislative level, such as a Congressional committee, or compliance with an environmental impact report (EIR), requires the attention of executives.

By comparison, the costs imposed by market institutions are delegable. Employee benefits are administered by full-time staff. These costs have the characteristics of regulation and litigation. They are specific to a market location and jurisdiction, and not tied directly to the productivity of the firm.

The cost of the health plan is not the direct responsibility of the CEO. The employee benefits manager and the personnel and human resources department cover the added paperwork. The CEO must respond immediately to a lawsuit. The executive, fearing for the loss of personal assets, over-responds. More time is spent on a lawsuit that affects the executive personally than on the business of the company. Similar arguments arise with regulation. Health care costs do not require an immediate response. Their magnitude, lack of relationship to the productivity of the individual employee, and specificity to a location suggest their importance in the cost of doing business. This chapter examines costs imposed by the market on doing business. There are no laws in the United States requiring the provision of health care benefits by employers, although some initiatives have been proposed.[2]

The state of Massachusetts has mandated health care for all residents, commencing in 1992. All firms with six or more employees in the state are required to contribute $1,680 per year per employee for coverage if there is no alternative health plan offered.

Firms provide benefits because of market pressures specific to a location. Competitors offer health insurance to employees. Two federal programs, Medicare and Medicaid, cover the elderly and the poor. The demand for protection against unforeseen risks, the risk of loss of employment earnings with illness, and favorable tax treatment cause competitive firms to offer health benefits.

The examination poses worrisome conclusions for U.S. business in control of health costs. Firms that offer full health benefits are obliged to do so by market pressures, at the risk of losing employees. These firms employ more skilled workers and pay above-average wages. Other firms, employing less skilled workers, do not offer health plans. Health care providers, given a worker population that includes some uninsured, shift costs to firms with insured workers.

Large firms subsidize small firms, and those employing unskilled labor. In societies where there is public provision of health care, all firms share equally with ability to pay, through tax system financing. Health care costs impose inequities between firms within the United States in their ability to compete. The Bureau of Labor Statistics reports that benefits have increased at rates double those of basic wages. Benefits have been argued to be entitlements, and firms have no more success than the government in controlling their increase in cost.[3]

HEALTH STATISTICS

Total Expenditures

There has been an increase in the absolute and relative level of health care expenditures in the United States. As with the legal system, medical expenses are growing more rapidly than output as a whole. Table 7.1 lists health care expenditures.

In 1965 the United States spent $205 per capita on health care, and $2,135 in 1988. In 1965 about 6 percent of gross national product was allocated to health care, rising to 9 percent in 1981 and 12 percent in 1988, with projections of further increases in share.

The increase in the expenditure on health has both a quantity and a

Table 7.1
Health Care Expenditures, United States, 1965–88

Year	Expenditures ($b.)	Per Capita ($)
1965	41.9	205
1970	75.0	349
1975	132.7	590
1976	150.8	665
1977	170.2	743
1978	190.0	822
1979	215.1	921
1980	248.1	1054
1981	287.0	1207
1982	323.6	1348
1983	357.2	1473
1984	391.1	1595
1985	422.6	1721
1986	458.2	1837
1987	498.9	1973
1988	544.0	2135

Source: United States Health Care Financial Administration.

price dimension. There is a health care component of the Consumer Price Index (CPI). For 1981–87 inclusive, the health care component increased faster than the CPI in each year, with an average differential of 3 percent. Health care usage rose. There have been increases in the number of doctors and doctor visits per capita. The relative share of health care costs in the value of gross national product has increased.

Outcomes: Health Statistics

Despite the high proportion of total output allocated to health care, the United States does not have appreciably better statistics in health outcomes than other nations. Infant mortality rates are listed in Table 7.2.

Infant mortality rates are higher for the United States than for other developed nations. The infant mortality rate is higher than in either Australia or Canada. Accounting for racial composition, the United States has an infant mortality rate similar to that of the other two countries. Race does not necessarily account for the entire differential. Blacks have lower income than whites on average. Some of the differential arises by selecting effectively on income. Children born to low-income mothers in Australia and Canada have higher-than-average mortality rates.

Increased medical expenditure does not necessarily result in improved health standards. In 1975 the United States spent 8.4 percent of its GNP on health care, but West Germany spent 9.7 percent, Canada 7.1 percent, and Britain 5.6 percent. The low relative expenditure in

Table 7.2
Infant Mortality and Doctor/Population Ratios

	Infant Mortality Per '000 Live Births	Doctors/'000
Australia	9.6	1.9
Canada	9.1	1.8
United States	11.2	1.7
White	9.3	
Black	19.2	

Source: Organization for Economic Co-operation and Development, and National Center for Health Statistics.

Britain is attributed to control on hospital expansion. Public health provision provides countervailing power in restricting usage, demand, and fees.

Price and Income Elasticities of Demand

There has been extensive examination of health care and costs. By comparison, the implications for business have received limited attention. There appear to be three problem areas here.

First, expenditures on health do not appear to alter health status, and the firm receives limited dividends on its expenditures. Infant mortality is relatively elastic to income; increases and improvements in income reduce death rates at young ages. Adult mortality is less responsive to changes in income. Higher income may be associated with a more risky life style and with stress and tension. For prime-age men and women (aged 16 to 64), those likely to be employed, income does not affect mortality rates. The number of physicians per capita, expenditures on health care, and medical inputs and facilities all do not appear to affect health outcomes. This conclusion applies to a small increase or decrease in these interventions. A large reduction in medical inputs is likely to affect health outcomes.[4]

From 1930 to 1960 age-specific death rates have fallen, though the improvement is concentrated in younger age groups. Explanations given are improved child nutrition, vaccines, the presence of antibiotics and penicillin, and the lower birth rate. The lower birth rate permits parents to invest in child quality rather than quantity. Since 1960 age-specific death rates have levelled off, notably after very young ages, and have actually increased in some categories. Expenditures on technologies such as organ transplants and lasers have resulted in costs for firms and no change in observed medical consequence.

The U.S. experience is similar to that in other countries, of a reduction in infant mortality, with only marginal changes in mortality of other age groups. In these statistics the United States lies only in the middle of industrial nations, despite the relatively larger expenditures.

Second, the demand for medical care services is unresponsive, or inelastic, to both price and income. For firms this conclusion implies that there is limited potential cost saving to altering deductibles and coinsurance. A 1 percent increase in income of the patient results in an increase in demand for medical care of between zero and 0.5 percent.

An exception is for those aged less than 15, who have an income-elastic demand for medical services.[5]

Prime-age men and women have an income-inelastic demand. For this group, as income increases, there is a demand for health care as for other goods. The opportunity cost of time, in transportation to appointments, and as a patient, acts to reduce demand. For children, this opportunity cost is lower. This combination of effects has a ratcheting effect on demand at firms offering coverage of dependents. Increased income causes an increase in medical visits and care of dependents. These children are healthier, but the employee producing the services for the firm is not.

The price elasticity of demand is also low, and ranges numerically between 0 and -0.5, with zero frequently obtained. A 1 percent increase in the price of health care paid by the user patient has no effect on demand. The firm is unable, or has limited flexibility, in controlling health costs by shifting the burden to the employee through deductibles and coinsurance. A large part of the price of medical services is the opportunity cost of time of the patient. The low income elasticity suggests that the use of conventional markets has limited capacity for cost control.

Third, increases in capacity, of both physicians and hospital beds, increases demand. A 1 percent increase in the number of physicians results in a 0.3 to 0.5 percent increase in the medical demand. There are several explanations for this phenomenon. As there is more capacity, the search, travel and waiting time of patients and their opportunity costs are reduced, and demand increases. Supply creates its own demand, in the suggestion of follow up visits and long term treatment. There is permanent excess demand, in that the price charged the user is below equilibrium. An increase in capacity is immediately absorbed by the market.

The employer cannot count on medical cost increases being repaid in increased productivity, health status, or duration with the firm. The firm may benefit if employees are freed of the risk and worry of medical costs. The firms are vulnerable to increased costs for dependents, for whom health care is a normal good, whose consumption increases with income. The prospect for cost containment at the firm level, through shifts of premium costs to employees, is limited, given the low price and income elasticities of demand. With continuing increases in capacity, usage levels increase, and so do costs.

Capacity, Supply, and Prices

An increase in the capacity of the medical system, and the supply of medical professionals, should reduce the price of the services, leading to a saving for payers of insurance premiums, including firms. In addition to receiving little benefit in healthier employees, there is no cost saving for an increase in capacity. Three explanations have been advanced for this phenomenon.

First, the market for medical services is in perpetual excess demand. The price of a visit to a physician or hospital is held below the market-clearing equilibrium level. The price restriction is because of custom and spillover from price control in public plans, and from restrictions by third-party reimbursers. Demand exceeds supply at the prices charged. Any increase in supply, of either physicians or hospital beds, does not reduce the price, but only reduces the excess demand. The observed price of health care increases even as supply rises.[6]

Second, visit costs are reduced by increased capacity. The cost of a visit to the user is the sum of direct and indirect charges. The direct charge is the net amount payable by the patient, in deductible and coinsurance. The indirect charge is the sum of commuting and waiting. The firm pays other direct charges, in the insurance portion. An increase in supply of physicians and doctors reduces the indirect cost of a patient visit, by reducing commuting time. Indirect costs are the largest part of total costs for the user. The price to the user declines, and demand increases. Firms, receiving no saving per visit, find total costs of insurance increasing with the additional visits. This hypothesis argues that the market works, when the total price of a visit is included.

Third, supply creates its own demand.[7] Medical specialists have more information on procedures than do patients. There is an asymmetry in information. There is an incentive to suggest medical intervention. An increase in supply may decrease demand in the short run. In the long run, demand is shifted outward by the increased capacity. The intensity of usage of medical services increases.

The argument is that medical professionals recruit customers. Individuals lack the information to determine the type and severity of illness. They cannot choose appropriate medical treatments and interventions. They defer to specialists, who have an incentive to suggest treatment. Specialists (here physicians) perform more tests, encourage return visits, and see more patients, even while population growth is relatively low.

Health Insurance

The United States is unique among industrial nations in that the bulk of its health insurance for the working age population is carried by private providers. These private providers are third-party insurance companies, hired by firms to offer health care services. In 1847 the first private health insurance company in the United States was established, the Massachusetts Health Insurance Company of Boston. Firms do not usually self-insure in offering to pay all health costs.

The government role in health insurance exists at the federal rather than the state and local levels. Commencing in 1966, Medicaid offered health insurance for the poor. For those over 65 Medicare is offered as part of the Social Security program. In 1967, 83 percent of those aged under 65 had health insurance. By 1980 only 80 percent of those under 65, and 62 percent of those over 65 had coverage.[8] The reduction of coverage among those over 65 is caused by the crowding out of private insurers by Medicare.

EMPLOYER INCENTIVES AND HEALTH CARE

Employer-paid benefits are subsized, since employees do not include them in taxable income. Employers are permitted to deduct the expenses in computing taxable income of the firm. The employee is restricted in choice over goods, by having to take compensation in kind through medical care. Some employees have a limited demand for health and other benefits.

Employees demand group health insurance because individual insurance is expensive. There is a saving in cost when the firm delivers a group of employees to an insurer. Pooling creates economies of scale and saves in the transactions costs of marketing, administration, and servicing that apply to individual accounts. Employees are risk averse. They seek to avoid high medical bills and loss of work time. This risk aversion leads to a demand for health insurance. The price is reduced by having the firm act as an agent, because of tax and pooling considerations.

Risk aversion implies that an individual pays a premium to avoid the potential of high medical costs, by buying insurance. All else being equal, the employee accepts a lower after-tax income, but the health insurance premium is paid from before-tax income.

These demands, from the tax subsidies, risk aversion, and economies of scale, lead employers to offer medical benefits. Indemnity plans include a deductible, requiring the employee to pay a certain total dollar amount before payment from the plan. The employee coinsures, by paying a percentage of the total billing. The total contribution of the employee is limited, providing coverage against catastrophic medical bills.

The employer pays benefits as part of the compensation package. The benefits of health insurance are relatively skewed. A small number of employees receive a disproportionate share of the total benefits. The firm is not likely to deny employment application or continuing coverage to those who are chronically ill, or to those who have a higher statistical likelihood of illness. Incidence of illness varies by both race and sex. Antidiscrimination legislation and acceptable notions of equitable treatment require that age, race, and sex not be used to establish compensation differences. All employees who perform the same work are paid the same, regardless of race, sex, or age. The firm bears a cost, if some demographic groups have higher rates of illness than others. Data on variation in death rates are indicated in Table 7.3.

Blacks are three times as likely in the general population to have AIDS as whites. The cost of pregnancy implies an expenditure associated with hiring a female employee. A male may have been present for the conception, but the firm incurs an additional cost in hiring a female. Employees without dependents subsidize those with dependents. If gay employees have few dependents, even when the risk of AIDS is included they can be less expensive to hire than employees with families. There are implications for other benefits in the compensation package.

Table 7.3
Death Rates per 100,000 Population, 1985

	Cancer	Diabetes	Heart Disease	Stroke
Black males	231.6	17.7	301.1	60.8
Black females	130.4	21.1	186.8	50.3
White males	159.2	9.2	244.5	32.8
White females	110.3	8.6	121.7	27.9

Source: National Center for Health Statistics.

The first $50,000 of term life insurance is not a taxable benefit if paid for by the employer. There are differences in accident and premature death rates by age, race, and sex. Black men have a lower life expectancy on average than white men. Death rates from accidents per 100,000 population in 1985 are 66.2 for black men, 21.9 for black women, 51.8 for white men, and 18.3 for white women. The cultural emphasis on personal and physical risk taking causes males aged 16 to 25 to have higher death rates than females. Since the firm is not charging a higher life insurance premium for males, they are subsidized by the females. The third-party insurer charges the employer a higher life insurance premium for males, but the salary of males cannot be lowered to compensate.

The firm cannot discriminate on the basis of race or sex in hiring. Some of the differences in disease rates by age, race, and sex are associated with income and poverty status. A firm recruiting a graduate electrical engineer is searching in a pool of relatively homogeneous workers in health risk, although all the variation need not be eliminated.

More of a problem is the overusing worker. The statistical differentials based on demographic characteristics can be objectively documented. The practical differences in health care cost by race or sex are liable to be reduced when employees have similar skills. The overusing worker of any race, sex, or age nominally performs the job but consumes a large quantity of medical services. The employee is not negligent in the discharge of duties, but because the distribution of medical benefits is skewed, this employee is costly.

Some areas such as psychiatric care have a cultural demand. Health plans have been obliged to place limitations. Some workers have preferences for frequent visits to a medical facility, whether a doctor's office or a hospital. Other workers have little preference for such visits. Where these differences in preferences for other goods are not subsidized, the employer need pay little attention.[9]

What the employee chooses to do with after-tax income is a personal matter. Even this statement is too strong, as the employee who engages in hang-gliding as a pastime poses a health risk to the plan. In response to the overusing worker, the third-party insurer is obliged to increase premiums. This is not a solution, since preferences, as opposed to the risk of random illness, are imposed on others. Suppose two workers are equally productive and are paid the same salary. In health benefits they are paid the same access, but one worker has a greater taste for this right. The employer has different costs for hiring the two workers, but is unable to adjust salaries.

If all employers in the same industry have medical plans with similar characteristics, the worker with the low taste for medical care cannot go to another firm. Another firm cannot offer a package with more direct compensation and fewer medical care benefits. Competition for workers establishes the package, and the well worker is as risk averse to large medical bills as the sick worker. Medical differences affect productivity. The sick worker tends to use personal days and sick leave, and the well worker is less likely to use them. The firm is able to dismiss the sick worker for lower work effort, but discharge for medical reasons presents legal problems and affects morale.

The firm is in a dilemma. The medical plan subsidizes workers who may have below-average productivity at the expense of those who have above-average productivity. The life insurance plan pays off workers who die early, from whom the firm loses output and production. These benefits do not reward productivity, and may reward slothfulness, preferences for medical care, and other perverse incentives that do not contribute to output within the firm.

The government is not, through regulation, requiring the firm to offer medical insurance. Rather, it is the market that mandates employee benefits such as health insurance. The firm not offering these benefits suffers a loss of employees to competitors.

Patient Dumping

In patient dumping, uninsured or underinsured patients arriving at private hospitals are denied care, and transferred to public hospitals. If private hospitals engage in patient dumping, they are accused of failing to live up to their obligations, discriminating against the uninsured, and risking complication by a delay in medical intervention. If they see the uninsured patient, they are providing free or *pro bono publico* medical attention. This cost is covered by the remaining patients of the private hospital.

Many health benefit plans cover the employee and dependents. With an increase in the number of two-earner couples having separate health plans, the complexity of reimbursement is increased. Resort has been made to rules of thumb, such as the birthday rule, where the primary carrier is determined by the member of the couple born earlier in the year. The primary carrier for a two-earner couple pays first on a claim.

Case: J. C. Penney

J. C. Penney, as is typical with large, national employers, offers a comprehensive health and dental package to employees. The benefit package, including the health and dental plan, increases total compensation of employees. A high percentage of the work force is female, who are employed in clerical and retail sales. On average females earn less than males.

Spouses of Penney employees are entitled to health and dental coverage as dependents. These spouses of Penney employees tend to be husbands.

Penney is the victim of employee dumping by the spouses of employees, and by other employers. The spouse of a Penney employee is free to take any job, including one that pays no health benefits. The reservation wage at which the spouse accepts employment is lowered relative to competitive potential workers. Penney is subsidizing employees at other firms.

There is a corollary. Spouses in jobs where the compensation is largely in direct salary, such as self-employment or direct sales, send their partners to work at J. C. Penney. These workers accept lower salaries in exchange for the medical benefits. Penney receives a tradeoff in employees, largely female, who are willing to work at lower salaries. Whether the subsidy from the employed spouse exceeds that to the nonemployed spouse depends on the local labor market. In markets with low unemployment rates, Penney pays the going salary. While continuing to offer medical and dental benefits as part of its national compensation package, it offers a salary competitive with local retailers.

In tight labor markets, where unemployment is low, Penney subsidizes other employers, and the spouses of employees. In slack labor markets, with high unemployment, it subsidizes spouses, and may be able to obtain employees more cheaply. In either case, there is employee dumping, where health care obligations are shifted from one employer to another. Since the Penney plan covers dependents other than spouses, the cost of the dumping can be substantial. The spouses of Penney employees generally receive higher salaries than their partners. Employers of spouses of Penney employees are subsidized. Even if they pay higher wages, they are not obliged to offer health plans.

The response was to restrict health coverage to spouses earning less than the Penney employee. The subsidy to high-wage nonemployees is removed. Many of these spouses had medical plans at their employment. Penney and the other employer were paying premiums for the same person, causing duplication of coverage. Duplication of coverage has expanded, given the increase in the number of two-earner families. The incentives for employee dumping are reduced but not eliminated. A spouse can work for a low-wage employer not providing health benefits and be covered.

The duplication of benefits makes it expensive to hire either member of a married couple. One solution is not to cover dependents in the health plan, but this restricts the number of available employees. If both spouses are covered at both jobs, two employers are paying twice for the same people. The firm cannot recover these costs from the employees. A single employee cannot be paid more than an employee with dependents. The costs are absorbed or shifted to customers.

The counter-argument to the Penney position is that the modified benefits package is discriminatory. Some employees and their dependents receive full coverage, while others do not. Paradoxically, the employees receiving the full coverage tend to be highly paid males in managerial positions. A Penney manager receives full dependent coverage if the spouse is not working or is employed in a low-wage job. A female store clerk married to a non-working male receives full dependent coverage. A female clerk married to a male custodian earning more, but with no medical plan of his own, does not receive full coverage. The Penney employee is covered, but not the spouse.

Consider a location where there is one dominant large employer, surrounded by smaller firms. The large firm offers full benefits, including a health and dental plan. The smaller firms do not offer this plan. Instead, they employee dump their health obligations by hiring spouses of employees at the large firm. The large firm is subsidizing the smaller firms.

One solution is to restrict health care coverage to the employee, with no extension to dependents. With coverage of dependents, those with large families are subsidized at the expense of those with small families. The firm is receiving only the output of the worker, but pays a larger health care premium for the worker with more dependents. The firm risks losing the productive employee with dependents.

HEALTH CARE COSTS

Benefits are not treated as taxable income to employees, but are deductible business expenses for employers. The firm spending $1 on employee benefits has the alternative of $1 in cost of wages and salaries. To the employee, the $1 of nontaxable benefits is worth $1 net, while the \$1 of income is worth $(1-t)$ cents, where t is the marginal tax rate, combining federal, state and local rates. The combined marginal tax rate is

$$t=t_f+(1-t_f)t_s$$

where t_f is the marginal federal tax rate, and t_s is the state and local marginal rate. State taxes are deductible in calculating federal tax liability. An employee in a 28 percent federal and 10 percent state bracket has a combined rate of 35.2 percent. The firm has a tax incentive to provide health benefits, pensions, subsidized parking and transportation, food, and term life insurance to its employees. Other benefits include tuition reimbursements and prepaid legal plans.

To the extent that benefits are not taxable, the return to the employee is higher than on a dollar of salary. If the firm reduces the compensation package, there is a saving in cost. Compensation taxed at different rates creates a demand for firms specializing in benefits consulting and human resource management. Firms require more sophisticated personnel and payroll departments to administer the benefits programs.

Prior to the Tax Reform Act (TRA) of 1986, the highest marginal rate of federal taxation on earnings was 50 percent. This rate has been reduced to a maximum of 28 percent.[10] The tax reform removed many low-income taxpayers from the rolls. A California resident had a top rate of 11 percent, reduced to 9.3 percent. For most wage earners, marginal rates of tax have been reduced.

The reduction in marginal tax rates reduces the price of having the employer offer a benefit. The employee has more incentive to take compensation in salary. Since benefits require more cost in administration than salary, the firm has a greater incentive to pay direct salary. At the top combined federal rate in California, the price of a benefit such as medical services was 45.5 cents per dollar. This price has been increased by tax reform to 65.2 cents. The $(1-t)$ cents in after-tax salary is spendable on any product or service, while the \$1 in benefits is restricted.

Perverse Incentives

With third-party or employer reimbursement, the price to the employee user is below the opportunity cost of the medical care resource.

The underpricing arises because the employee has only the time cost of using the service, and a coinsurance component a fraction of the bill submitted by the provider. The opportunity cost of the employee is the greater of the two components, since time and output at work are lost. These opportunity costs may be lower for a nonworking spouse covered as a dependent.

When any good or service is underpriced, the employee tends to overuse it. Since decision making is out of the hands of the employer, it is difficult to control costs. The firm facing an increase in the price of paper clips shifts to another supplier, provided that there is no monopoly in the industry. The firm is not making the usage decision directly on medical care, though restrictions apply. Conventional indemnity insurance does not provide for direct purchase of the medical care of the employee.

The demand for medical care is relatively unresponsive to the price charged, but relatively responsive to the recommendation or referral of physicians. Increases in copayments and deductibles limit demand, but their ability to do so is constrained. The firm cannot regulate the number of medical facilities and doctors in the market. This makes costs difficult to control, since the price mechanism does not work directly.

There is a cross-subsidy from healthy employees to those who are sick, have many dependents, have spouses at firms that offer limited benefits, and have preferences for medical attention. Health plans were developed when there were fewer two-earner couples. The growth of two-earner couples, with overlapping medical coverage, leads to over-insurance and paperwork. Firms freeload on others offering generous coverage. If both members of a married couple are covered for dependents, the firm with the more generous coverage is likely to receive the claims. Executive time is spent on enforcement unrelated to production.

There are no controls on the supply of medical care, in the delivery of medical services, hospital capacity, or number of physicians. When firms are unable to control the availability of services, they are vulnerable for cost increases through caseload and claims.

The legal system, with the attendant cost of litigation, spawns defensive medicine and increases in premiums to pay for malpractice insurance. Some suppliers of medical care have higher costs than others, but employers usually cannot restrict the choice of provider. An employee on a conventional health plan may resist transfer to a health maintenance organization (HMO).

There are accounting restrictions. Regulations proposed by the Financial Accounting Standards Board require firms to disclose the unfunded present values of their long-term health liabilities. Firms reflect on their financial statements the present value of unfunded pension obligations to retired employees, and the present value of health benefits payable to retired employees and their dependents.

Cost Shifting

With a mixture of private and public health care, there is cost-shifting to those with greater ability to pay. Hospitals and medical practitioners have legal and moral obligations to provide care on demand regardless of ability to pay. After the fact, collection of unpaid and unpayable bills is difficult. Realizing this risk, suppliers quote medical prices exceeding the minimum average cost of the service. The excess profits on these patients provide a reserve to cross-subsidize those unable to pay the bills.

The latter group falls into two categories. Federal Medicare and Medicaid, restrict reimbursement, such as in the diagnosis related group (DRG) program. The provider is not able to collect all costs. Those not eligible for public health care rely on their own resources. Included are the self-employed and those working for low-wage employers. Suppose low-wage employers reduce labor costs by not offering health benefits. These employees are subsidized by providers. The subsidy is covered by charging higher prices to firms paying full health costs. This group mainly contains large firms. Large firms, through the tax system, are paying the cost of operating public hospitals. These facilities are used by employees of competitors not paying health benefits.

High-wage employers, including large companies, and those employing relatively skilled workers, are obliged to offer medical care by market pressures. Low-wage employers are free riders. High-wage employers are not only bearing the cost of medical expenses, but are "overcharged" to subsidize those with limited resources. With large employers paying excess medical expenses, differentials in costs for hiring a worker in the high-wage sector rise relative to the low-wage sector.

It becomes more difficult for large firms to increase employment. This medical cost alone may account for the relative or absolute lack of employment growth in large companies since 1970, while total employment has increased. Firms rely on suppliers for purchasing other inputs, as in the Japanese manufacturing case, or use franchises to delegate the employment decision.

In this "creaming," high-quality employers offer extended health benefits and the federal government offers restricted benefits to some members of the population. Other employers offer no or limited benefits. The high-quality employer subsidizes the health care of the rest of the population.

Federal Medicare covers those over 65, who are eligible for Social Security. This group includes many who are able to contribute to medical costs. Veterans of the armed forces with an honorable discharge are able to receive free medical treatment from Veterans' Administration hospitals. The poor are covered by Medicaid.

Firms and employees pay for these programs directly, through corporate and personal income taxes, and payroll taxes for Social Security that finance Medicare for the elderly. If government expenditures exceed revenues, firms and workers pay in the liability for the budget deficit. These payments arise as with any public program. The difference is that in addition, employers offering full coverage subsidize other medical care demanders. They cover the differential in unreimbursed billing for those unable to pay, or where there are restrictions.

The full care providing employers are in a quandary. They can reduce or eliminate coverage. Since competitors continue to offer coverage, they risk losing their best employees. Employees continue to value the medical care benefit. The benefits are tax free, the risk aversion to random high bills is unchanged, and pooling lowers prices.

The employer has the alternative, if continuing to require skilled labor, of shifting to locations with public provision of health care. Such a transfer implies a location outside of the United States, alone among industrial nations in having no universal medical care coverage. The firms save the cost of coverage, and reduce the internal bureaucracy in the employee benefits department. While there are higher direct taxes to pay for universal coverage, there may be a saving. If the public agency acts as a countervailing power against the monopoly supply of providers, the cost of supplying medical care is reduced.

The evidence from Western Europe and Canada appears to support this contention. Medical care costs are not sufficient to engender relocation decisions, but the differences in production costs are considerable. General Motors estimates medical costs amount to $500 per car produced in the United States. Chrysler estimates that 90,000 vehicles a year must be sold to cover the medical costs of its U.S. workers.

In Canada, where there is universal medical care, and free trade in automobiles since the Canada–United States Auto Pact of 1964, there are no corresponding costs. Marginal tax rates on corporations and individuals at the Canadian federal level have been reduced to rates similar to those in the United States.[11] The tax burden of paying directly for medical care is not necessarily higher. The firm is not exchanging an obligation to the third-party insurer for an obligation to the tax authority. Canada offers favorable production costs as compared with the United States; there is an incentive to locate production there, for the saving in medical care benefits.

Health Maintenance Organizations (HMOs)

A large part of the growth in medical care coverage in the United States is accounted for by HMOs. These organizations provide health care benefits at little or no direct charge at the point of service, to the user. There is no coinsurance payment by the user, and frequently no deductible.

The employer is billed directly at a charge per employee or dependent. In exchange for the elimination of billing, patients are restricted in choice of provider. Services are provided at the facilities contracted with or operated by the HMO. In some cases choice of individual practitioner is restricted. Individual employees are precluded from membership. This increases the attractiveness of the HMO, since the firm provides the pool of clients.

The HMO has characteristics that suggest reductions in employer health costs. There is a focus on preventive medicine. Coverage of routine check-ups and lifestyle changes is included, reducing the risk of later high-cost illnesses. Medical staff including physicians are hired on a salary. The salary reduces the incentive for the physician to generate large billing levels, and to increase patient visits. By self-selection, the HMO attracts the less entrepreneurially inclined physician, another factor in cost control. The lower risk of salary fluctuation, and elimination of bill collection, reduces the expenses of the physician. By charging a fixed price, employers know in advance the total cost of coverage.

Despite the growth of these organizations, and the increasing percentage of workers covered, the rate of growth of medical costs in the

United States has not slowed. As the number of HMOs increases, it is possible that the quantity of medical interventions increases.

There are administrative problems. HMOs may engage in cream-skimming or adverse selection. Adverse selection arises where one provider has bad risks, such as less healthy workers, and the other provider has good risks. Younger, healthier workers opt for the HMO, while older workers remain in conventional indemnity plans. Many firms, particularly large employers, cover their retired work force. The retired are covered by topping up Medicare. The conventional plan has health care risks, of older employees and the retired. Since the conventional indemnity plan cannot subsidize its unfavorable client base, it shifts the cost to the firm. Health costs increase even as workers belong to the HMO. The competition between conventional providers and HMOs need not reduce health costs, but increases them. The firm has the paperwork associated with dealing with several providers.

Conventional plans increase rates as their patient load shifts unfavorably, as an appropriate market response. This market reaction increases the attractiveness of the HMO to the healthy worker, and the tendency to leave the conventional plan. This vicious cycle, termed the "doom loop" by insurers, guarantees a worsening adverse selection, with the attendant cost being absorbed by the firm and its customers.

One alternative is a preferred provider plan. In this plan, a conventional insurer contracts with certain suppliers. If these are used, the employee pays a lower price. This plan has market incentives to control costs. The preferred provider plan does not eliminate the doom loop.

Emphasis in the HMO is placed on cost control. Since there is no variable charge, profit on a user is made only by nonintervention. A profit-maximizing HMO has an incentive to avoid expensive treatment. By comparison, costs of such a treatment are recovered by a conventional plan. Since the marginal revenue to the HMO from treatment is zero or low, these plans attempt to minimize cost by nonintervention. These incentives may not always square with those for health. The elimination of forms and paperwork, and the zero user charge, increase demand.

Retired Workers

Health care coverage for the retired is complicated by accounting provisions. The FASB has increased oversight of unfunded health care liabilities, particularly where employers top up Medicare health plans for retirees. The topping up plan for the retiree pays the difference between actual billing and Medicare reimbursement. This opens the firm to liabilites in health care billing, except that it cannot obtain output from the retiree as compensation.

Any payment of a medical benefit above a premium collected is a subsidy, paid by either the remaining employees or the firm. If the product has a price-inelastic demand, the firm shifts some of this cost to consumers. The firm incurs a cost without a corresponding contribution of output. FASB regulations propose inclusion of the present value of the medical care cost of retirees as a liability on financial statements. On the balance sheet, the firm would estimate the future cost of providing retiree benefits. These regulations provide improved accounting information, and communicate to shareholders and managers the extent of the potential liability. Where firms have a relatively young work force, such as in high technology, the current dollar cost of a provision to pay the medical benefits of retirees is low. Unless workers are induced to leave the firm prior to retirement, there is potential for a large medical care liability.

Excess Capacity

It is increasingly expensive for a patient to stay in a hospital. Third-party insurers, conventional and HMO alike, and employers making direct reimbursement, have an incentive to discourage hospital stays. The requirement of second opinions on surgery, prospective permission from the insurer for hospital admittance, and increases in the paperwork burden associated with stays are attempts to discourage inpatient visits, and to reduce the stays of those requiring hospitalization.

Hospitals are institutions with large fixed costs in overhead, and relatively low variable costs. The costs of the nursing, medical, and ancillary staff and physical plant are largely fixed. If bed occupancy rates are reduced because of restrictions by insurers on stays, hospitals increase the charges for days actually spent. Hospitals are forced to reduce volume, but if there are returns to scale, the average cost per patient day increases. The hospital is moving upward on its average cost curve, and must spread its fixed costs over fewer patient days.

The response of the hospital is to increase per diem charges and fees for usage. Health plans with outpatient facilities provide competition for hospitals. The competition reduces demand for hospital beds.

When workers face lost time and wages, they are reluctant to accept long-term hospitalization. Community pressure prevents hospitals from reducing and closing facilities, so the increase in average cost is borne by the remaining customers.

Medical Personnel

Between 1977 and 1987 the number of physicians in California increased by 49 percent, but the population increased by 22 percent. Despite an increase in the doctor-to-population ratio, the average income of doctors increased. In 1987 the average annual income of all physicians after expenses was $119,000. In obstetrics and gynecology, after paying office expenses including liability insurance, the average was $280,000. Data on surgical procedures suggest that increased capacity is related to increased utilization.

Surgeons and other medical practitioners gravitate toward metropolitan areas and the East and West Coasts. The rate of elective surgery is higher in urban than rural areas, despite the higher ratio of surgeons to population in metropolitan centers.[12] Increased supply is associated with an increase in prices for procedures. The price index of surgical visits in the Pacific states is 111.1 and in the Middle Atlantic states 121.9, with the United States at 100. If the surgeon-to-population ratio continues to increase and becomes more concentrated, there may be increases in the rate of surgical procedures and in their prices.

With debt burdens on graduates of medical schools, there is pressure to generate billings. The cost of becoming a doctor is the sum of tuition and the foregone earnings while in medical school, and during internship and residency. An increase in the cost of becoming a doctor attracts the more entrepreneurially inclined, as opposed to those less willing to generate billings. This cycle from higher costs of medical school to increased billing volume ends in costs borne by firms and insurers.

Nursing is a female-dominated occupation. Until the growth of labor market opportunities for women, nursing was a field that attracted a steady supply of applicants. Competitive pressures from other jobs have reduced the supply of women entering the nursing profession, and caused many in it to leave.

Nursing has unfavorable job characteristics. Hours are long, and shifts inconvenient. Working on some wards is unpleasant. There is little glamor in the profession; dress-for-success strategies do not lead to career advancement. Contacts on the job are people facing unpleasant circumstances. Immigration restrictions reduce the prospects of seeking nurses from overseas.

The combination of these factors and monopoly power in some hospital unions has increased salaries. The derived demand for medical care as capacity increases implies an increased demand for nursing and other support staff. In 1988 Kaiser Permanente, the largest HMO in California, was offering $40,000 in annual base salary to nurses, and up to $50,000 annually for nurses with experience. The Stanford Hospital matched this salary package after a strike threat. In 1988 Centinela Hospital in Los Angeles was offering $30,000 to start, and up to $70,000 for a nurse with five years of experience.

Medical delivery is relatively labor intensive. It is difficult to substitute for nurses in patient care. As the demand for health care increases, there is an increased demand for nursing care. The increase in the population above 75 years of age presages an increase in the demand for full-time nursing attendants.

Technology

Regulation and litigation lead to restriction in the supply of medical technologies and pharmaceutical treatments. In exchange, regulatory agencies permit longer patent lives and more monopolistic protection. Litigation, more likely in medical products and service delivery, increases the price of medical services, medical insurance, and the cost of providing employee benefits. New technologies do not necessarily reduce the cost of medical care.

New drugs and technologies are expensive, since the producers cover high research and development costs, spread over up to ten years of testing. Tissue plasminogen activator (TPA) by Genentech and azidothymidine (AZT) by Burroughs Wellcome are such cases. The monopoly effect and the costs of regulatory delay implied that the initial price of AZT in March 1988 was set at $2,200 per treatment, as noted earlier.

AZT was approved by the FDA under its 1-AA program to speed up approval of anti-AIDS drugs. In 1987 AZT was marketed with an annual dosage cost of $8,000. Federal programs made AZT available to those with 1987 annual income of less than $22,000.

The cost of new drugs is high because of the learning curve pricing used by high-technology firms. There are high fixed costs of research and development (R&D) and low variable costs of production. The production site is footloose, located to minimize costs globally. R&D costs, particularly in pharmaceuticals, are specific to a location. The regulatory structure of the FDA governs the cost of producing drugs in the United States. The average cost of production declines with the quantity produced. The first users are charged for the fixed costs of the R&D. If the R&D expense is increased because of regulatory delays, and the monopoly granted the supplier, the price of the drug is increased.

In a full coverage plan an employee user has a low access price for health care. The deductible and coinsurance are a small percentage of the price of AZT for an AIDS patient. The firm, through the insurer, pays the high cost of the technological innovation. Full coverage medical plans pay for R&D in the medical and pharmaceutical industry. These high costs arise not only for drugs and pharmaceuticals. A heart transplant in 1988 cost $125,000. Some transplant operations, such as for kidneys, are fully covered by the federal government. Others are shifted to insurance. If insurers refuse coverage claiming transplant procedures are experimental, the costs are absorbed as overhead by hospitals. These overhead charges are ultimately reflected in fees to other users of the hospital.

The Uninsured

In the United States, of those less than 65 years of age in 1980, almost one-fifth had no health care coverage.[13] Among white Americans under 65, 14 percent had no coverage, and 4 percent more were covered by Medicaid. Among black Americans, 22 percent had no coverage, and 17 percent more were covered by Medicaid. The problem of the uninsured is more acute for medical services than in other markets. In the market for apples, those not paying any price do not retain any right to consumption of apples. For medical care the situation is different. A sick person cannot easily be denied treatment. The distribution of coverage is indicated in Table 7.4.

An uninsured person is not denied access to health care. Health care providers are legally and socially restricted from turning away the uninsured. Employers providing limited or no health care benefits engage in free riding. Paying limited benefits, these employers can pay higher direct salaries to their employees. If they pay the same salaries as other employers offering full benefits, their labor and business costs are lower. Uninsured workers tend to be employed in low-wage jobs, and to

Table 7.4
Health Insurance Coverage, United States, 1986, by Race

	White	Black
Private Insurance	79.1	57.0
No Coverage	14.0	22.6
Medicaid 4.0	17.4	
Other 3.0	3.0	

Source: National Center for Health Statistics. For the population under 65 only. Those over 65 are covered by Medicare through Social Security, or by private insurance with previous employers. Other includes public health insurance for civilian and military employees.

be relatively unskilled, less healthy, and to have a greater claim on medical care.

High-wage workers, with higher opportunity costs of lost time from ill health, tend to be insured. This causes an adverse selection, where the good health care risks are already covered. Any expansion of employer plans to those not covered is more expensive than for the average person. Among nonworkers, the public provision of Medicare and Medicaid is covering relatively high cost clients. The burden of the uninsured is shifted from some employers to others, and to taxpayers. Of the uninsured aged under 65, half are employed. Firms with health plans are cross-subsidizing those with no health plans.

Demographic and Social Factors

The fraction of the population over 65 years of age is increasing. Many of these persons retain health insurance from the employer, combined with Medicare. The age group over 65 has the highest consumption rate of health care. With low access prices to users, and no public authority controlling costs and availability, there is little structure to ration demand. Medicare for over-65s limits hospital reimbursement. This restriction increases the pressure on firms to cover the differential between the actual billing and the Medicare reimbursement. A public restriction is shifted to private employers.

Malpractice insurance, with low-priced access to courts in some states, causes increases in medical fees. Florida and New York have high prices for malpractice insurance, high rates of lawsuits against doctors, and high fees in obstetrics and gynecology. Malpractice insurance is estimated to account for 11 percent of total medical costs, and increases the practice of defensive medicine, with excessive testing to avoid suits. The increases in prices and testing are absorbed by firms paying the posted prices for medical benefits, and avoided by those not providing benefits.

Another social phenomenon is diseases striking those in prime earning years, notably AIDS. AIDS is not a more expensive disease per case than others involving long-term suffering and medical intervention, such as cancer. The two population groups at high risk to AIDS are intravenous drug users and male homosexuals. Among the male homosexual cases, those typically contracting the disease are whites aged between 25 and 40 years of age, frequently employed in professional capacities. The loss of output to society and a firm has a high present value. The firm loses the capital value of output for the length of time the worker would have been employed. Society loses the capital value over the remaining working life. The health plan pays costs of medical intervention over a protracted period.

The other, and more rapidly growing category at high risk is the intravenous drug user, where the disease is communicated by the sharing of hypodermic needles. The disease is spread by mothers to babies. These AIDS patients, predominantly young blacks and Hispanics in inner cities, increase health care costs. When they are uninsured, they are treated at public hospitals funded by taxpayers. These facilities cannot deny access, so costs for society are increased. Firms in the United States bear the cost, both in lost output and health care, for those stricken with the disease, and in the tax burden to treat the uninsured.

The United States is not alone in facing the demographic and social conditions of increasing health costs. The age composition of West Germany and Japan is more unfavorable, with an increase in the population of elderly. The cost of caring for the elderly is publicly shared through the tax system. In the United States the cost is shared piecemeal. Medicare covers those over 65 to a limit. Some firms cover their retired employees, and others shift the cost to society.

Preventive Medicine

The healthy employee who engages in preventive activity, through exercise, dietary control, and avoidance of stress or other high health risk behavior, is not rewarded by either corporate or public health plans.[14] Health plans pay if the employee is sick, and do not pay if the employee is well. There is little incentive through a health cost saving to remain well or to invest in wellness. Health plans tend not to invest in preventive medicine, and some restrict routine checkups and physical examinations. Where firms offer preventive programs, relatively healthy workers participate, so there is self-selection. The well workers participate, and the sick do not. Some plans have imposed restrictions on prescription drugs such as for hypertension, but this implies more heart attacks.

The diligent employee who avoids substance abuse and high-risk behavior, and exercises regularly, reduces the risk of high-cost illnesses. This activity reduces costs for the third-party insurer and for the firm. There is no monetary benefit to the employee other than in personal health. This employee cross-subsidizes another who engages in higher health risk activity. The healthy worker is less of a claimer on the medical benefits pool, and actuarially pays for the illnesses of other workers. Investments in preventive activity, such as exercise, are not usually reimbursed by the employer. Expenses are borne by the employee from after-tax income, while health care payments are made from before-tax income.

Preventive activity as a prescription is more difficult for the patient user to accept, since it requires changes in preference structures or lifestyle. It is less financially rewarding for health care providers, since there is a reduction in the use of direct treatment. Health care providers have no direct incentive to prescribe preventive activity. Users have no financial incentive to accept it. Both provider and user have incentives to opt for drugs and medical intervention. This cost is shifted to insurers and firms.

Medical Supplies and Paperwork

The use of prescriptions provides an easy way out for health care providers, since swallowing a pill is easier than a regime of daily exercise. Prescriptions permit the medical system to obtain repeat business. While prescription drugs are not necessarily abused or over-prescribed, there is no incentive not to prescribe. Hard decisions arise with prescriptions of life style changes. Easy decisions arise in filling pill prescriptions.

Some surgery has a high value added, such as hip replacements or hernia operations. Other tests are more expensive, but the demander, the patient-user, is unable to determine whether such testing is necessary.

An anecdotal story is told of a state administration. It had been elected on a pledge to reduce expenditure and waste in the state welfare department. Changes in rules, reduction of benefits, the attempt to induce work from the able bodied, and provision of day care failed to put a dent in the caseload. The reductions were effected by introducing a complicated 17-page application form. The number of claimants was reduced, but equity suffered by eliminating many who were technically eligible. This regulation mechanism appears to be the only weapon available to firms in controlling costs. The administration of benefits is in the hands of external third parties. The increase in the requirement of paperwork acts as a tax to induce restraint in usage of medical care facilities.

SECURITIES TRADING AND THE FIRM

Market forces do not increase costs solely in health care. In equity markets, firms offer Employee Share Ownership Program (ESOP) plans as a major benefit to employees. Employees have their compensation restructured, away from salary and toward stock options. Market trading strategies shift overall risk from one group of stockholders to another. The group liable to receive the shift in risk is employee shareholders.

There are two types of shareholders, institutions and individuals. Included among individuals are employees, executives, and officers of a publicly traded firm. Institutional investors are short term oriented, with relatively high turnover rates in their portfolios. Individuals are long-term investors with lower turnover rates. Individual investors who are employees have legal restrictions on trading stocks from ESOPs.

Institutions have access to trading strategies such as index arbitrage and portfolio insurance that require capital not available to most individuals. These strategies increase the risk of trading, of not trading, or of ownership of stocks. The risk is shifted to individual investors. The institutional investors are hedged against declines in the value of the firm, but individual investors not using these strategies are not hedged.

Index Arbitrage

Arbitrage capitalizes on differentials between prices of similar products in different markets. Index arbitrage arises on the difference between the spot price of an index of stocks, and the current price of the futures contract on the index. If the price of the futures contract is below the cash price of the index, the arbitrageur buys the futures contract and sells the stocks in the index. If the price of the futures contract is above the cash price, the futures contract is sold and the stocks are bought.

Index arbitrage is fully hedged against price movements in either direction. The position is taken by buying or selling individual stocks, groups of stocks, or stock index funds. Some index funds require written notification before shifts can be made, restricting these activities. Others have restrictions on holding short positions. When the stocks or the indexes are sold short, the funds are invested in interest-bearing accounts. The proceeds, invested in such instruments as short-term Treasury bills, provide a return to the index arbitrageur not always available to the individual short seller.

With index arbitrage the institutional investor takes advantage of differences in current prices of an index of stocks and a futures contract on the index. There are two prices, one for the index P and the other for the futures price of the index F. An equilibrium relationship between the index and the price of its futures contract is

$$F_e = (1 + R)P$$

where R is some riskless interest rate, such as on three-month Treasury bills, and F_e is an equilibrium price. The market price of the futures contract F may be above or below F_e. Suppose F is below F_e. The index arbitrage investor buys the futures contract, which requires a relatively small cash margin, and sells the stocks in the index at P. The cash received from the short sale is invested at the riskless rate R.

If at any date prior to the maximum three months to expiry the futures contract exceeds F_e, the arbitrageur is guaranteed to make F_e, a profit over the F invested.

Portfolio Insurance

Portfolio insurance minimizes the risk of a large movement in stock prices. The portfolio insurer, upon a movement in the price of the index, takes an opposite position in the futures contract. When the price of the index falls, the insurer sells the futures contract. Further falls in the price of the index are insured by being able to buy the contract at a lower price.

If a group of stocks falls in price, the portfolio insurer sells the stock index futures contract. If stocks prices fall further in price, losses are covered by the gains on the short position. Upon selling short the stock index futures contract, the cash received is invested in short-term interest-bearing instruments, such as Treasury bills. The portfolio insurer receives interest on this position. If H is the number of futures contracts held, then $H = H(P)$, where H is an increasing function of P.

A problem arises with the interaction between index arbitrage and portfolio insurance. Suppose there is a decline in the index. Portfolio insurers sell the futures contract on the index, reducing its price. The reduction in price causes the price of the futures contract to be below the cash market equivalent. Index arbitrageurs buy the contract and sell a basket of stocks in the index. The declines or increases feed on themselves.

More important is the division of risk between institutional and individual shareholders. Institutional investors are able, through index arbitrage and portfolio insurance, to lay off the risk of stock ownership. Even if there is no increase in the volatility of the price of stocks, the risk is transferred to those not using these techniques.

Individual investors include employees, with long-term horizons, and an immediate concern for the fortunes of the firm. The increase in risk of ownership of stocks is transferred to these employees. The employees risk capital loss. They are unhedged, and hold naked positions in the stock. Employees are distracted, and more likely to be disloyal. If the trading strategies reduce the risk of stock ownership in aggregate, and all the reduction of risk is not captured by the strategy, individual owners benefit. In a declining market the users of portfolio insurance and index arbitrage are protected relative to the naked owners, including the employees.

Employees may have a large proportion of their wealth in the ESOP. These employees have more risk in their portfolios, potentially affecting their work productivity and the performance of the firm. The decline in the stock price of the firm could become a self-fulfilling prophesy.

PENSION PLANS

Another source of market-imposed costs is pension plans. Firms in competitive industries offer pension plans to induce loyalty and longevity of employees. Pensions are particularly important where an employee has a firm-specific skill, such as senior management talent. The public sector, at federal, state, and local levels, tends to offer defined benefit plans, where the pension payment is a function of one or a series of years of salary. Competitive conditions oblige other firms in the private sector to offer comparable plans. A defined contribution plan entails the employer making payments with each paycheck to a pension plan. The contributions of employer and employee are invested, and used to purchase an annuity at retirement to fund the pension. The employee cannot be paid more than the amount in the individual account retirement fund.

There are differences in mortality and life expectancy by characteristics such as age, race, and sex. Women live longer than men, and whites live longer than blacks on average. Pension funds are precluded from discriminating on these characteristics. The 1964 Civil Rights Act prohibited discrimination in wages, and its terms have been applied to pension funds.

A firm hires a man and a woman of equal productivity, receiving the same output from the two workers. This firm, as is common in old-line manufacturing and in large corporations, has a defined benefit pension fund. The earnings during employment are the same, but the present value of the retirement benefits for the woman are higher, given her longer average life expectancy. The firm is not permitted to charge the woman higher contribution rates to the pension fund. This is prohibited by a 1978 U.S. Supreme Court ruling based on the 1964 Civil Rights Act. In 1983 the Supreme Court prohibited employers from paying women a lower pension.

The cost of hiring a woman of equal productivity to a man is higher, given the pension. A defined contribution plan is an alternative, but has the disadvantage of having no reward structure for loyalty and longevity. The absence of a pension plan may be unappealing to those expecting to live a long time. The firm cannot reduce the salary of the woman while employed, or increase that of the man above the woman. Either the employment of women is reduced, or the firm resorts to underemployment of women. In a large organization it may be possible for some workers to be paid less than the value of their productivity. These workers donate output to the firm if they are geographically immobile, if they are already paid above the opportunity cost of time, or if the job provides psychic income such as friendships.

Alternatively, the firm absorbs the cost, by having higher costs of production and higher prices. In a competitive market where all workers are paid the value of their output, the employer cannot shift the cost. The market imposes a cost of administering the pension plan, and there are transfers to women able to survive to retirement.

CONCLUDING REMARKS

Health costs are specific to a location. The U.S. firm producing in Canada does not require a health benefits manager, and does not pay premiums to a third-party provider. Some provinces in Canada have a levy for medical care premiums, but they are relatively low. With these shifts come inequities. Large firms have extensive benefit plans; small firms do not. Employee dumping arises, with the small firms shifting benefit coverage to large firms. It becomes more difficult for large firms to increase employment, since their cost of doing business is higher. There are prospects for cost control, although none appear to have produced substantial savings. The spread of HMOs controls costs, and permits firms to predetermine expenditures. There is self-selection in participation. Lower marginal tax rates reduce the advantage to employer and employee of benefits such as health plans. Cafeteria benefit plans, where employees choose packages, permit employees to determine allocation between medical and other benefits. Cash incentives are paid by some firms to those with low usage rates of medical plans. The employee dumping or shifting problems are likely to become more acute with the increase in two-earner couples.

There are practical and ethical issues. The employee with no dependents receives less in benefits than the employee at the same firm and salary with covered dependents. The firm receives the same output from the two workers. The firm cannot pay less to the employee with dependents. The spouse is subsidized, having a lower reservation wage for taking a job elsewhere that offers no medical benefits.

Employee benefits are not paid directly for the productivity of the worker. Frequently, the firm pays benefits to the worker taking advantage of institutional slack and goodwill, even if not technically committing infractions. Since firms outside the United States are not subject to the same type of cost, a problem of international competitiveness arises.

NOTES

1. This survey is based on 1987 data. It was conducted by the employee benefits consulting firm of A. Foster Higgins.

2. A national health proposal would require all employees working more than 17.5 hours a week to be provided with a minimum benefits plan.

3. In 1987 wage increases were 2.6 percent for unionized workers and 3.5 percent for nonunionized workers in private industry. Total compensation including benefits increased respectively by 3.9 percent and 4.0 percent. Benefits increased at a rate of 5.8 percent.

4. M. Grossman (1972) *The Demand for Health: A Theoretical and Empirical Investigation*, New York: National Bureau of Economic Research and Columbia University Press. Grossman conducts an interstate study of mortality. Per capita income and health care expenditures and inputs have no effect on mortality.

5. V. Fuchs (1986) *The Health Economy*, Cambridge, MA: Harvard University Press. The medical care variable is the number of general practitioner equivalent visits annually. The data are a cross section across states in 1966. With no variables other than income, the income elasticity is 0.3 to 0.4. A 1 percent increase in income increases visits by 0.3 percent.

6. M. Feldstein (1970) "The Rising Price of Physicians' Services," *Review of Economics and Statistics*, 121-33, has advanced this hypothesis. According to time-series data, the price elasticity of demand for physicians' services is positive, violating a law of demand. When the price of these services is increased, demand increases.

7. See Fuchs (1986) and R. G. Evans (1974) "Supplier-Induced Demand: Some Empirical Evidence and Implications," in M. Perlman, ed., *The Economics of Health and Medical Care*, London: Macmillan.

8. The source of the statistics is the *Source Book of Health Insurance*, of the New York Health Insurance Institute. Another factor in the diminishing relative coverage of working-age persons by health plans is the rising cost of health care and insurance.

9. The employer is affected by other preferences that affect productivity, such as smoking and substance abuse.

10. The Washington Business Group on Health is a corporate group attempting to control health care costs.

11. In 1988 there were two personal income tax brackets in the United States at the federal level, of 15 percent and 28 percent, and one corporate rate of 34 percent.

12. See V. Fuchs (1986: 146).

13. National Center for Health Statistics.

14. Vernon Coleman (1988) *The Health Scandal*, New York: Sidgwick and Jackson.

References

Reference to court decisions or testimony before federal and state legislative committees is made directly in notes. The references include texts, journal articles, and published material by research foundations.

Akerlof, G. A. "Labor Contracts as Partial Gift Exchange." *Quarterly Journal of Economics* 97 (1983): 543–569.

_____. "Gift Exchange and Efficiency Wage Theory: Four Views." *American Economic Review Papers and Proceedings* 74 (1984): 79–83.

Batra, R. N. *The Great Depression of 1990.* New York: Simon & Schuster, 1987.

Clermont, K. M., and J. D. Currivan. "Improving the Contingent Fee." *Cornell Law Review* 63 (1978): 4.

Danzon, P. M. "Contingent Fees for Personal Injury Litigation." *Bell Journal of Economics* 14 (1983): 213–224.

Danzon, P. M., and L. A. Lillard. "Settlement out of Court: The Disposition of Medical Malpractice Claims." *Journal of Legal Studies* (1984).

Fuchs, V. *The Health Economy.* Cambridge, MA: Harvard University Press, 1986.

Glazer, Nathan. "Toward an Imperial Judiciary." *Public Interest* 41 (1975): 118.

Hill, J. "Litigation and Negligence: A Comparative Study." *Oxford Journal of Legal Studies* 6 (1986): 183–217.

Jury Verdict Research. *Personal Injury Valuation Handbook.* Solon, OH: Jury Verdict Research, various issues.

Kahneman, D., and A. Tversky. "Prospect Theory: An Analysis of Decision Under Risk." *Econometrica* 47 (1979): 263–92.

Kakalik, J. S., P. Ebener, W. Felstiner, G. Haggstrom, and M. Shanley. "Variations in Asbestos Litigation Compensation and Expenses." Santa Monica, CA: Rand Corporation Institute for Civil Justice, 1984.

Kakalik, J. S., and N. M. Pace. "Costs and Compensation Paid in Tort Litigation." Rand Corporation, Report RAND/R-3391-ICJ, 1986.

Landes, W., and R. Posner. *The Economic Structure of Tort Law*. Cambridge, MA: Harvard University Press, 1987.

Lieberman, Jethro T. *The Litigious Society*. New York: Basic Books, 1981.

Lipson, A. J. "California Enacts Prejudgment Interest: A Case Study of Legislative Activity." Santa Monica, CA: Rand Corporation Institute for Civil Justice, 1984.

Manne, H., et al. *Medical Malpractice Guidebook*. Jacksonville, FL: Florida Medical Association, 1985.

McKinnon, F. B. *Contingent Fees for Legal Services*. Chicago, IL: Aldine, 1964.

Morita, Akio (with Edwin Reingold and Mitsuko Shimomura). *Made in Japan*. New York: Doubleday, 1986.

National Center for State Courts. *State Court Caseload Statistics: Annual Report*. Various issues.

O'Connell, Jeffery. *The Lawsuit Lottery*. New York: Free Press, 1979.

Peterson, M. A. "Punitive Damages: Empirical Findings." Santa Monica, CA: Rand Corporation Institute for Civil Justice, 1987.

Peterson, M. A., and M. F. Shanley. "Comparative Justice: Civil Jury Awards in San Francisco and Cook County, 1959–80." Santa Monica, CA: Rand Corporation Institute for Civil Justice, 1983.

Schotter, A., and J. Ordover. "The Cost of the Tort System." Starr Center for Applied Economics, New York University, March 1986.

Schwartz, M. L., and Mitchell, D. J. B. "An Economic Analysis of the Contingent Fee in Personal Injury Litigation." *Stanford Law Review* 22 (1970).

Sculley, J. (with John A. Byrne). *Odyssey: From Pepsi to Apple*. New York: Harper & Row, 1987.

Selvin, M., and P. A. Ebener. "Managing the Unmanageable: A History of Civil Delay in the Los Angeles Superior Court." Santa Monica, CA: Rand Corporation Institute for Civil Justice, 1984.

Sowell, T. "Lawsuits and Legal Visions." Stanford, CA: Hoover Institution, January 1987. Mimeo.

Spence, A. M. *Market Signaling*. Cambridge, MA: Harvard University Press, 1974.

Trubeck, D., et al. *Civil Litigation Research Project (CLRP): Final Report*. Madison, WI: University of Wisconsin-Madison Law School, 1983.

United States Department of Justice, Bureau of Justice Statistics (BJS). *The Federal Justice System*. Washington, D.C., July 1987.

_____. *Justice Employment and Expenditure 1985*. Washington, D.C., 1986.

United States Department of Justice, Tort Policy Working Group. *Report of the Tort Policy Working Group on the Causes, Extent and Policy Implications of the Current Crisis in Insurance Availability and Affordability*. Washington, D.C., February 1986.

_____. *An Update on the Liability Crisis*. Washington, D.C., March 1987.

Viscusi, W. K. "A Workmen's Compensation Proposal." In *The Tort Reform and Alternatives*. New York: Manhattan Institute for Civil Justice, 1988.

Index

ABOUT THE AUTHOR

PETER CHINLOY is on the faculty of the School of Business, Santa Clara University. He has also taught at the University of British Columbia, the University of Western Ontario, and the University of Southern California. He is the author of four books, and his articles have appeared in numerous professional and academic journals. Dr. Chinloy holds a B.A. from McGill University and an M.A. and a Ph.D. from Harvard University.